NO THANKS, I'M JUST LOOKING.

Professional Retail Sales Techniques
For Turning Shoppers Into Buyers

By Harry J. Friedman

KENDALL/HUNT PUBLISHING COMPANY
4050 Westmark Drive   Dubuque, Iowa 52002

THE FRIEDMAN GROUP
RETAIL TRAINING AND DEVELOPMENT

Post Office Box 92003
Los Angeles, CA 90009
(800) 351-8040 • (310) 645-7355 • FAX (310) 645-6241

DEDICATION

I lovingly dedicate this book to the people that I have met in retail. I hope this book can, in some way, pay back some of the knowledge I have gained from them. Foremost, I thank my family for their love while I continue to play the "Game of Retail."

ACKNOWLEDGEMENT

For six years I have wanted to put a book together on retail selling but it always took a backseat to being out in the field teaching it. Traveling a quarter of a million miles a year doesn't afford much time to write. Finally I met Jeff Davidson. He took countless hours of my audio and video tapes and put together a wonderful draft. Marlene Cordry, my right and left hand for the last seven years, along with my very talented staff, helped put the finishing touches to it. To my partner, Jon Dickens, thanks for all of your help.

I have always believed I am the result of all my yesterdays. Those days were filled, as I hope my tomorrows will be, with meeting people who have added so much to my knowledge. This book is a result of that learning.

It is sometimes very difficult to acknowledge or remember every source that goes into a book. If I have used a technique or an expression from someone else, it is because that is now what I believe. Sorry, and thanks!

CONTENTS

FOREWORD

Few professionals today have to respond as quickly to changes in consumer demand as does the retail sales professional. What sold like hotcakes yesterday may be dead stock tomorrow. Similarly, salesperson-to-customer retail sales techniques that may once have worked wonders in our fast-paced society now may lead to disastrous results, especially among sophisticated, street-wise consumers who have "heard it all" and "seen it all."

If you're using outmoded techniques or if you fail to understand the psychology of why people buy, your earning power, your career, and your well-being are in jeopardy. If you lack the proper tools and the techniques, the marketplace can quickly become a jungle that will chew you up and spit you out. In fact, personnel turnover in retail selling is among the highest of all industries or professions.

Enter Harry J. Friedman. Harry is president of the Los Angeles-based retail sales and management training firm, The Friedman Group. By his mid-thirties, Harry had already built his firm into one of the most successful training firms in the industry.

In his video programs and live presentations, which are in demand throughout North America and Europe, and now in this book, Harry strips away conventional wisdom about what it takes to be successful in retail selling. In its place, he lays down a foundation, rooted in proven and effective methods that he personally devised over decades of research, study and first-hand experience.

This book will save you time and endless hours of frustration. Harry is a master of retail selling and retail sales training, but more important, he is one of those gifted individuals who possesses a unique ability to convey his knowledge in an entertaining yet highly supportive manner. He enjoys helping sales professionals and they enjoy listening to him. Now, they will enjoy reading what he has to say.

Starting with what to do even before customers walk into the store, progressing through all the critical elements that lead up to the sale, and offering coaching through post-sales issues, Harry decisively spells out what you need to know to *increase your sales results every day, regardless of what you're selling.*

Harry wants you to succeed. In this book, he pulls out all the stops, offering both insightful instruction and compelling reading. He opens up his treasure chest of profitable procedures for interacting with prospects. Harry introduces key phrases, appropriate gestures and effective behaviors for getting the prospect on your side in a hurry. Further, he reveals what the customer is thinking, wants to see, and needs to have confirmed.

His understanding and explanation of customer psychology is, in a word, outstanding. Through dialogue culled from actual sales encounters, from the minuscule to the magnificent, Harry provides the essence of effective retail selling in today's world.

If you read this book, your sales career will take a turn for the better. I predict that you'll pore over the pages time and time again to squeeze out every golden nugget of Harry's knowledge. If you're in retail selling, or any other profession where favorably influencing others is important, you'll find that this book is more than an instructive guide, it's a chance to change your standard of living forever.

Richard Erhart
Former Executive Vice President
InterTAN (Radio Shack International)

INTRODUCTION:

You can't always buy right.
But you can always sell right.

No matter how unusual you think your merchandise is, how different you think it is from someone else's wares, the truth is that customers don't appreciate the same distinctions that you do and may regard what you have as just about the same as the next salesperson's. So, if your merchandise is not perceived to be substantially different from that found in other places, why will shoppers buy product from you instead of buying it from the store down the street?

It all boils down to *you*. Success as a salesperson depends entirely on *your* ability to open up customers, to communicate with them, and to satisfy their needs.

When people choose a doctor or lawyer, their selection is based only in part on that individual's education. Feeling that you can relate person-to-person is a major factor in choosing and staying with one professional over another. A good professional knows that an excellent education is only a small part of what goes into a prospective client's decision to use him or her. Reputations are built and practices grow as much because of "people skills" as because of technical skills.

There are no born doctors, lawyers, accountants or plumbers, and there are no born salespeople, either. People in business need technical, personal and business skills to succeed. Learning these skills is an ongoing process that changes as new information becomes available and new methods of doing things are developed.

Unfortunately, in today's retail environment, salespeople are professionals who often act like clerks. Clerks may do an adequate job of executing routine tasks at work, but they don't develop special skills, "go the extra mile," do their homework, or cultivate their customers.

Like clerks, salespeople have frequently let their "people skills"—and their technical skills—remain uncultivated.

In this book, we'll show you how to develop "people skills" and selling skills that will not only boost your income, but will also dramatically increase your job satisfaction. The first chapter, "The Precheck," covers the basics of what to do before the store opens in the morning; in a sense, getting your act together before you take it to the floor.

Chapter 2, "Opening the Sale," addresses the unconscious things salespeople have been saying to shoppers over the years, and offers a professional sales approach to speaking with your customers. It is frightfully true that too many sales-people have resisted doing their homework and refrained from any degree of preparation. This has resulted in ineffective probing and unenthusiastic demonstrations offered by ill-informed personnel. Chapters 3 and 4 cover the crucial skills of probing and demonstrating.

In Chapter 5, the "Trial Close," we'll tackle the professional salesperson's mandate to close the sale with a bonus of adding on to the sale.

In Chapter 6, we'll focus on the all-important skills of handling objections, followed by techniques for closing the sale in Chapter 7. In the past, salespeople have been happy with the hit-or-miss approach to selling, contenting themselves with intermittent closes and merely respectable sales. The professional salesperson goes for the close every single time with every single customer. We'll discuss in depth how you can do that using your own personal style.

Finally, in Chapter 8, we'll highlight how to use confirmations and invitations to build more sales, encourage repeat business and generate referrals.

As we proceed throughout the book, remember:

If you choose to say hello to a customer, choose to sell and satisfy that person!

CHAPTER ONE

GETTING YOUR ACT TOGETHER BEFORE YOU TAKE IT TO THE SELLING FLOOR

It is so very difficult to draw water from an empty well.

In a March 1989 article, Brian E. Kardon spelled out a new retail term called "consumer schizophrenia." He noted that it may be the most important revolution in consumer behavior since the mass-marketing movement in the 50s.

Simply put, the way people buy could be characterized as schizophrenic. For example:

You own an expensive imported car and go to a self-service gas station and pump your own gas.

You buy premium designer ice cream at the market and at the same time buy the house brand dog food or unbranded tissues.

You buy a custom-made suit and go next door and buy toys at discount.

Selling today is remarkably different than it has been in the past for two major reasons. The first is that people tend to be cautious about where they spend their money, wanting the best quality and the best deal. Second, at the same time that people are careful about spending, there are more consumer goods than ever and greater use of the mass media to advertise them. This, of course, fosters more competition for the customer's disposable income.

People don't really *need* a luxury car or a diamond bracelet, but they *want* that kind of merchandise, or desire to use it to express their love, or their excitement and joy over special occasions. There is, after all, something exhilarating about finding exactly the right gift for someone, or precisely the right piece for yourself. Your goal as a professional salesperson is to create a desire in your customers to want what you have. That is retail selling!

It is no secret that the ingredients for success as a professional salesperson can be summed up in three words:

Preparation
Preparation
Preparation

. . .preparing your emotional and professional self, knowing your merchandise and price structure, understanding what your competition is doing: these are all essential to successful selling.

The Not-So-Fun Stuff

In 1974, I became a pilot. Why? I have no idea. It just seemed like the thing to do. In studying to become a pilot, one of the first things I learned was to prepare for each and every flight by doing a "precheck" or pre-flight inspection. The precheck encompasses tasks basic to a pilot's safety, such as checking the gas and oil, making sure the compass is working, seeing that there are no dents or holes in the fuselage and making other fundamental checks that will keep the plane from falling out of the sky and resulting in pressed aluminum. It really sounded like a good idea to me.

Taking care of these essential items is what helps a pilot grow to a ripe old age. There's a saying in aviation: There are *old* pilots and *bold* pilots (a bold pilot referring to a pilot who gets into a plane without checking on the fundamentals), but there is no such thing as an *old, bold pilot*. Similarly, there are salespeople who flourish and salespeople who are foolhardy, but there are no foolhardy salespeople who flourish for very long.

Many salespeople only want to learn about the perceived "important" steps of selling, such as how to close, handle objections and add on. No one likes to do paperwork or stock work; those parts of the job are tedious. But every job has tiresome tasks, which simply have to be done in order to succeed.

In retail selling, performing repetitive and seemingly painstaking, boring "precheck" chores lays the groundwork for your success on the floor.

Professional retail selling starts with preparation and knowledge; these, in turn, give you self-confidence and control over the selling process.

Some of the elements of preparation take only a few minutes but have to be done every day. This means that you need to arrive at the store well before your shift begins, so that you will have time to prepare your "plane" for takeoff.

Some elements of preparation require a greater investment of time, and may have to be undertaken after work or on days off. Long-range preparation, which we will discuss later in this chapter, will help you with your overall approach to your work as well as with your daily precheck.

Whether daily or long range, preparing yourself will help you be the best professional retail salesperson you can be, and make you less likely to face a "crash landing" when you are with a customer.

3

CUSTOMER SERVICE POINTS

Retail is a funny business. We all know that companies that offer high levels of good customer service not only stay in business, but in most cases flourish. Those who don't . . . don't. Simple, right?

Wrong! I am consistently amazed as I travel around the world at the number of retail salespeople who offer little or no service to their customers. We all have certain stores or restaurants that we like to frequent because of the service we receive from people who work there. The waitress at the local coffee shop who calls you by name and knows exactly what you mean when you say, "The usual, Alice." The dry cleaners clerk who knows exactly how you like your clothes cleaned and pressed *and* makes sure that they are done that way every time, on time.

I recently went to buy a gift for a close friend. This particular store was very busy so I had the opportunity to observe the salespeople in action prior to making my purchase. There were two salespeople working behind the counter. One was a middle-aged woman, very well dressed and, on first glance, very professional. The other was a younger woman, in her early 20s. She was not dressed to the hilt like her co-worker, but did have a professional appearance.

As I waited, I observed customer after customer walking away frustrated by the first woman's actions. She didn't smile, gave short, terse responses to questions, etc. In contrast, the younger woman was ringing up sale after sale. She had a smile from ear to ear. She used the customers' names. She took the time to gift wrap the purchase of a man who was in a big hurry. Who do you think I chose to buy from? No question! There is no substitute for good, basic customer service—period.

I have included 20 customer service points that, through the years, have been proven the most effective in ensuring that your customers feel relaxed and comfortable with you and your store. Try them. Dare to be different.

1. Satisfy Every Single Customer

Retail can become a trap. If you don't sell the customer you're talking to, there is likely to be another one that you can sell, which will make life worth living again. The trap is never being forced to confront why you didn't make the sale with the first customer. It is always more fruitful to learn from your mistakes than your victories.

Can you look me straight in the eye and tell me without blinking that you have gone for the sale or gone the extra mile with every single customer you have started a conversation with? I doubt it. Shoppers are not and have never been an interruption of your work: they are your work. Heck, they're the only reason for you to show up in the first place.

I truly believe this is one of the reasons why I have been successful. I could care less *what* people were going to buy, just that they did. Each one was an opportunity to expand my customer base. And besides, I get cranky when I don't go to the register a lot. The question is: "How good are you?" The answer lies in your ability to turn shoppers into buyers at a high percentage, not just how many dollars you put into the register.

From management's perspective, hundreds of thousands of dollars are spent in merchandise, location and advertising. It flat out makes sense to try to sell everyone who comes in, doesn't it? Additionally, as a financial consideration, there is a cost attached to driving each customer in the door. For example, in the piano or hot tub business, it could run as much as $200 in advertising and promotion costs per shopper to get them to come in. In traditional mall stores, the figures may be as low as $10. In either case, for each person you do not sell, that amount is added to the next customer who comes in. So if you didn't make the sale on our piano shopper, that $200 cost is added to the next shopper in. That next selling opportunity now costs you $400! You can see how easy it is to go out of business because you didn't try to sell everyone.

2. Keep Personal Problems Off the Floor and In A Drawer

When *you're* the customer in someone else's store, you expect prompt assistance and courteous treatment—an indication that you are important. Your customers deserve, demand and expect no less than that, regardless of how you feel personally on a given day.

It's not always easy to adjust your mood, especially if you had a flat tire on the way to work, your teenage children picked an argument with you last night, or you're in the doghouse with your manager. Nevertheless, your customers are entitled to the same "very best" from you that you are entitled to when you are in someone else's store.

Shoppers can't be expected to care about your personal problems, and if you let your "bad day" show through, you will leave a poor impression of yourself and of your company. This ability to perform regardless of problems has always been a benchmark of the professional.

3. Don't Congregate on the Selling Floor

Picture this: You're in the store on a day that's so quiet you've been listening to the clock tick for amusement. About mid-morning, you and your colleagues stand around guarding the register and get involved in a heated debate about last night's big game. You're so caught up in this vital discussion that you continue talking, although you see that a shopper has come into the store.

She doesn't look like a promising customer; she's not focused on any particular item, seems to be browsing aimlessly, hasn't asked for help and her hair isn't exactly right. You and your colleagues continue your conversation, the shopper roams through the store for a while and then leaves. Is this any way to run a railroad?

It's easy to get involved in a conversation with other salespeople, especially when things in the store are slow. However, that's not what you're there to do. When customers need help, they feel uncomfortable about interrupting salespeople who are obviously engaged in personal or even business conversations. A customer who is uncomfortable about interrupting may wind up feeling angry about being ignored.

You can't always control when customers will come in and you certainly can't bring them back if they leave feeling displeased. You *can* always find time to "chew the fat" with your friends and colleagues, but let's be clear: the selling floor is not the appropriate place to do it, particularly when there's a customer in the store. You never want customers to feel that your conversations with fellow sales staff are more important than *they* are.

The rule for today and every day is: when you're on the floor, there's nothing more important than your customer. In theory and in practice, the customer always comes first. There should be an understanding among all floor personnel to stop the conversation when anyone walks in, regardless of how important it is.

4. Acknowledge Every Customer's Presence

Every customer who walks through your door needs to be greeted in some way; at the very least a simple "Hello." Doing this conveys a friendly feeling to your customers, making it clear that you know they're waiting, and suggesting that you soon will be available to assist them.

Customers don't always seek out a salesperson when they need help. Perhaps it's because shoppers feel embarrassed or because they don't want to disturb a salesperson who looks busy. Or maybe they just don't like salespeople, period. Even if you're occupied with something else, giving your customers quick recognition while they wait for your attention helps them develop a positive attitude toward you and your store. Acknowledging customers makes them feel welcome and lets them know you're glad they came into your store.

To really understand this point, think of the last time you had a party at your house. You're in a conversation with one of your guests, and out of the corner of your eye you see a friend come into your house. Even if you can't leave the current conversation, I'm sure that you, with either eye contact, a nod of the head or a wave of the hand, acknowledge the presence of your latest guest to your home. Should your business home be any different?

Noticing customers also has a beneficial side effect: it is the number one deterrent to theft in retail stores. When you make it clear that you have observed the presence of people who have come into your store, they are less likely to attempt to steal any merchandise.

5. Never Qualify Customers

Have you ever met someone you didn't like right off the bat? Or, on the other hand, met someone you liked as soon as you said hello? This chemistry is very important in the world of selling.

Did you ever judge a customer upon entering your store as someone who probably wouldn't buy, most likely couldn't buy, never will buy and can't even spell "buy"?

Okay, I admit it. I have always looked at customers and prejudged whether they were going to buy and how much I thought they would buy. I still do it, with a twist. There may be only one difference between the way I act now and the way some salespeople still act. Now my opinions don't have the slightest effect on the way I treat or serve customers. I have been burned too many times earlier in my career to continue making judgements based on appearance. There is nothing like dropping perceived losers only to have a rookie salesperson, who doesn't know "you should judge people," sell them the store. The top ten list of prejudices are, in no particular order:

1. Quality of clothing
2. Age
3. Gender
4. Foreign accent or language
5. Local accent
6. Race or religion
7. Mannerisms
8. Facial features
9. Weight
10. Hair style

And one more that didn't make the list may be the biggest prejudice of them all: the customer who comes in three times a week and has never bought anything.

The fun I have now is to see if my initial reaction is right. It's a game. I make my guess when they first walk in, then sell like crazy no matter what. After they leave, whether they bought or not, I see if my initial reaction was correct. If you're a saleaholic like me who wants to sell everyone, you might want to play the game like I do.

6. The Invasion of the Customer's "Personal Space"

Take special care to sense what your customers regard as their "personal space." Some people are outgoing from the first words you exchange; others feel uncomfortable when you get too close—physically or otherwise. Before you become too friendly, you have to earn the customer's trust. Don't gamble.

Personal space may be defined as the closeness you are comfortable having with someone, physically and verbally. With some, their physical personal space extends about two feet. With others, being in the same store with you at the same time is too close. In opening the sale, we will talk a lot about physical distance and its implications.

Verbally, there is something you really want to avoid so you don't violate your customer's personal space. Don't use your name or ask customers for theirs at the beginning of a presentation. Your customers may feel that their names are very personal. The name exchange at the beginning may very well be too pushy for a lot of shoppers who would like to remain anonymous until they determine if they like what they see. However, during probing or the demonstration, it becomes very important. Timing is everything.

I use the "friendly test" to get the customer's name and get an indication of how formal or casual I should be. Offer your name first and see if the customer reciprocates. Simply say, "By the way, my name is Harry," and wait for a response. There are three possible responses. If the customer says, "I'm Jane," she is comfortable with your calling her Jane. If she says, "I'm Ms. Smith," you can call her by name, but you had better be a little more formal. Or, she might say, "That's nice." What you've got here is a customer that is ultra resistant and you have your work cut out for you. If she doesn't offer her name in return, you must respect her personal space.

The point is that some people are just more casual and comfortable with people right out of the gate. I know I would never answer "Mr. Friedman." I'm just "Harry" to anyone I meet. We had a company party to celebrate our tenth year in business and I invited my dad to come. As I was introducing him to my staff, someone said, "Nice to meet you, Mr. Friedman." My dad replied, "I'm not Mr. Friedman. That's my father!" I guess it's genetic.

As we'll examine in opening and probing, perception is a big part of positive communication, and you can learn a great deal about customers from body language and the way they respond to your comments and gestures. Many a sale has been lost by violating a customer's space—unconsciously.

7. No Sir! No Ma'am!

It would be typical of me to dispute a long-time tradition of retail salespeople, wouldn't it? Well, it's time to do it again! Avoid using "sir" or "ma'am."

In a recent quest to buy some dishes, I went to a store that is considered to be a little more upscale, influenced by the false perception that in a smaller boutique type store, I would receive better service. After selecting a pattern and finally tracking down a salesperson, I asked if I could get everything I wanted today.

The reply was "I'll check, sir!" I cringed. The salesperson returned and said, "No sir, we don't have all of the pieces in stock, but we can order them for you, sir!"

I can't stand being called "sir" by anyone at any time for any reason, period. Is it me, or is it a common reaction? Every day I wake up I feel 18 until I look in the mirror only to find it isn't so. I know people are just trying to be polite, but I've asked thousands of people sitting in my classes if they like being called sir or ma'am, and the vast majority— like 95 percent—all hate it, too.

It makes younger or middle-aged people feel older and reminds more mature people of the age they're trying to hide. And it's particularly condescending when a salesperson older than you calls you "sir." Trust me, drop the "sir" and "ma'am." Just be courteous and polite and leave it at that.

8. Be Empathetic—Not Sympathetic

You are in business to sell and serve customers, not open a psychology practice. Crafty customers have all sorts of stories they can tell to trap you into believing the price is too high...or that they need something different, or that you have to make exceptions. Sympathy is feeling sorry for the way your customers feel. Empathy is understanding how they feel (like walking in their shoes), but not buying in. You can see the danger in not knowing the difference. Many a sale was lost by a salesperson who felt so sorry for a customer that he or she didn't feel it was right to make the sale.

If a man is vacillating about whether he should spend money on an item in the same month that taxes are due and the kids need new shoes and the dishwasher just bit the dust, most salespeople sympathize, tell the customer they understand, and express their hope that he will come back again when things are better. I, on the other hand, would empathize by saying, "I know what you mean. Whenever I feel like I shouldn't spend money, the only thing that seems to make me feel any better is spending more. Why don't you go for it?"

9. Listen to Your Customers' Ideas—Not Just Their Words

Customers may not always know the correct or technical terms for the merchandise they want. Salespeople often take great pride in knowing industry jargon. This can create a dangerous clash. As an example, a customer once asked me what type of VHS she had to buy to play my sales training video tapes. It would have been easy for me to say the tapes are *VHS format* and the machine is a *VCR*, but why? Why make her wrong? Of course, it is important to let her know the difference—but after I make the sale, not before.

Words are tricky. There is no guarantee that two people hearing them believe they mean the same thing. By knowing your products and really listening, you can decipher what your customers mean and serve them without "being right" or losing a sale.

It can also get you out of some tight spots. I did some sales training for a group of furniture stores once and visited one of the stores right after the session. Of course, the salespeople challenged me by handing over the very next customer who walked in. I had never been in the store, I didn't know where anything was, I was completely out of my element and ill-equipped to serve any customer. But I had eight salespeople eager to watch the master die right in front of them. I had to take the challenge.

This lady walked right up to me and said she was looking for a davenport. I'd never heard the word davenport in my life. I'm a native Californian and apparently this was a midwestern way of saying sofa. I said, "Well, that's great. What type of davenports have you seen before that you really liked?" She said, "Well, I really want a seven-foot one this time . . ." and I immediately ruled out lamps as a possibility. Ideas, not just words. Don't forget. (By the way, I sold her!)

10. Use Words to Express—Not Impress

Each industry has developed words to better describe things and to prevent misunderstandings and confusion. For example, in the computer business there are words like "megabyte" and "ROM." In jewelry, there is "inclusion" and "refraction." These words make it very easy to communicate with people in the same industry. They are, however, words that may confuse customers who are not up to snuff with industry jargon. Most of the time, customers won't ask what the words mean if they are used in a presentation. This would show a weakness and vulnerability. So instead of clearing up the misunderstood words, they leave.

Suppose a guy decides to take up jogging. He hasn't bought a pair of athletic shoes in over 15 years and has no idea of how expensive and technologically complex they have become. He tries on a pair and the salesperson mentions they have an EVA midsole. The customer hears the word EVA and immediately feels unqualified to make a decision.

He leaves and finds out what kind of jogging shoes his neighbor wears, and then buys the same kind from someone else. If the salesperson hadn't taken for granted that every customer knew what EVA meant, he could have explained its benefits and been the friend who helped the customer make the buying decision, instead of his neighbor.

Keep your language simple and understandable. If you need to use an industry word, make sure you explain it at the same time. For example: "This computer has 20 megabytes of memory. That means it can store up to 20 million characters."

There are two exceptions to this rule: 1) salespeople who are women or young looking men, and 2) technically educated customers.

Society thinks that women don't know anything technical. (Nothing could be further from the truth.) So women need to establish themselves as experts by throwing a little jargon around early in the presentation. And I don't know if I want to spend $5,000 on an entertainment system from a guy who doesn't shave yet. If he starts talking about total harmonic distortion, I not only like it, but I trust him more.

With customers who are technically educated, speak at their level or slightly above it occasionally to gain their respect. But all the while, you should also be complimenting them on their knowledge. "This is great. I finally have someone to talk to who knows what I'm talking about!"

11. Customers Love Power

There is a certain feeling of power customers have when walking into a store. They ARE the customer and therefore feel that they are in charge. For years, they have heard the old adage "the customer is always right." Well, you and I know that they are not always right. But we need them more than they need us, so we will make them right. Customers are people. And people can be obnoxious, rude, loud and can push every negative button you have. I must have lost thousands of dollars telling these people how wrong they were.

Now, I believe I have the solution. Sell these people about twice the amount of merchandise they came in to buy. I am on the floor to serve without an opinion of my customer. After all, I'd rather be wrong and rich than right and broke. Wouldn't you?

12. Never Interrupt Your Customers

If you are anything like me during a presentation, you can't help occasionally being so enthusiastic that you interrupt your customers to make a point or correct them on their thinking. The negative side effect to this is a possible lost sale.

People think and feel they are important. And they are. When you interrupt, you are saying that they are not important. Wait your turn, and you are more likely to make the sale. I used to put a Band-Aid around my finger so tight that it hurt just to remind myself to shut up and let the customer talk.

13. When Your Customers Are Talking, They're Buying

The average person speaks at a rate of 125 to 150 words per minute. You are physically capable of hearing upwards of 1,000 words per minute. So when someone is talking to you at 150 words per minute, what do you do with the other 850 words left over? You probably get distracted and concentration becomes very difficult. I suggest that you take on the burden of listening more than talking and you will have a more involved customer. So whether you believe in evolution or creation, it's interesting to note that you have two ears and only one mouth! Research shows that when customers are talking, they are, in a sense, buying. It's when they are quiet that you're in trouble.

14. Conversations Should be Two-Way

Have you ever tried to get into a conversation with a customer who finds talking an almost impossible thing to do? Quality questions have always driven a fine presentation. Your ability to ask pointed-enough questions to draw out your customer is essential. When all else fails, the easiest way to get a customer to start talking is to close the sale. I know this sounds ridiculous, but no matter where you are in the conversation, this puts the burden on the customer to tell you how he or she feels about your offer to sell.

For example, you're making great points: "Another great thing about this . . ." No response. "And another thing . . ." Silence. You finally resort to "Shall I wrap it up?" Zoom! They start talking in a flash.

15. Get Your Customers to Like and Trust You

Bob is at a party and the host introduces him to someone. . .

"Bob, this is Mary. Mary, this is Bob." And instantly Mary goes on a verbal tirade. "Bob, you wouldn't believe how my day has been! I started off this morning with a flat tire and that was only the beginning. . ." and on and on. After a while, as Bob politely gets out of the conversation, the host asks Bob how he liked Mary. Bob's answer is "Yuck."

The host then introduces Bob to someone else. "Bob, I would like you to meet Sara. Sara, this is Bob." Bob says, "Hello," flinching and fearing another Mary. Sara says, "Bob, how are you?" This time Bob goes off and talks non-stop for 15 minutes without Sara saying a word. A little later, when the host asks Bob how he liked Sara, he responds, "She was terrific." The host asks what she said, and Bob responds with, "I don't know, but I like her." The moral of the story? The easiest way to get your customers to like you and trust you right away is to let them do the talking. After all, you already know what you know. What the customers know is important and your job is to get them to verbalize it.

16. Always Look Professional

As soon as customers enter your store, before anything has been said to them, they have begun to form an opinion of the premises, the merchandise and you. Shoppers' feelings may be affected by many things beyond your control, such as their frame of mind, personal problems or preconceived ideas about your company. That is why it's especially important that you do your best with the things that *are* in your control.

Both the store and the people offering service within it must have an appropriate personal appearance. Obviously, a store that looks like it's in need of straightening is not as inviting as a store in which the displays and showcases are neat, clean and bright. The salespeople, too, need to be well-groomed, dressed appropriately and sporting a friendly and welcoming manner.

I got my first job in retail when I was 15 1/2 years old. It was at the height of the long hair craze and I had to make a choice between peer pressure and sales. I really wanted the long hair, but I wanted money more. So I can understand how youngsters don't want to give up trendy looks or clothing for a minimum wage job.

Not long ago, I had to deal directly with this problem at a sporting goods retailer that employed about 80 percent high school age kids. We had an open forum about the dress code at the store and I said, "I don't care if you have orange spiked hair as long as it's in a perfectly straight and neat row!" They got the point. The postscript to the whole story is that we finally let them decide on what the new dress code should be. They came up with black pants and ties. Go figure!

I look at it this way: Look and dress as professional as you would like to be. I have a tendency to give customers respect and therefore dress up a little more than normal in retail. I have never believed that you should dress like your customers to make them feel more comfortable. Salespeople in such industries as bicycles, diving and sporting goods are famous for this. One bicycle store I visited had salespeople wearing cut-offs, tennis shoes and T-shirts advertising rock bands I'd never heard of before. That's great if you're selling to someone who is under 20, but what if I want to come in and drop $1,500 on a bike? You've got to dress to offend the least number of people possible. It is, at the very least, worth experimenting with.

I also know that if I were to return to a retail floor permanently right now, I would always wear a red bow-tie and red suspenders. That would make me different. I'd have a distinctive look. Then even if the customers didn't remember my name, they'd at least be able to ask for the guy with the red bow-tie. What makes you stand out?

17. Stay In Control

Left to their own devices, customers will run you around the store causing all sorts of confusion, most of the time resulting in a NO SALE. Control can be maintained in any sales presentation if the following things are in place:

- Total understanding of the selling process.
- People knowledge.
- Product knowledge.
- Complete knowledge of what you have in stock and where it is.

"Winging it" is the problem. When you wing it you have a very difficult time controlling the sale, and making your customers feel comfortable enough to buy.

18. Certainty is the Key

The amateur *wonders* if customers are going to buy. The professional *knows* they are going to buy and it's only a matter of what and how much. Certainty comes from the accumulation of knowledge and experience. I know a lot of people in sales with 20 years of experience. Unfortunately, it's really one year of experience repeated for an additional 19 years. Others grow each year and learn from from mistakes and the acquisition of new knowledge. People who choose to shop with you have a conscious or even a subconscious desire to own what you are selling. So unless you have a crystal ball, assume everyone is going to buy and start your journey into finding out what it is.

19. Sell With Enthusiasm Whether You Love It Or Hate It

Selling merchandise you like is certainly easier than selling anything you dislike. You may feel such personal enjoyment about certain items that you never want to show alternatives, or you may be bored by the same old stock and only want to show what's new.

What matters is what the customer wants, period—not what you like or think is best. The moment—the second—you can sell the merchandise that you personally dislike with as much enthusiasm as the merchandise you love, that is the moment you can begin to call yourself a professional.

You may love an item in your store because you're engrossed by the process of getting it from the raw state into the wonderful shape it assumes on your shelf. As an example, you may think it's fascinating that diamonds are formed after millions of years in the depths of the earth, and go through miners, cutters, wholesalers and distributors before they appear on the gorgeous hand of your customer.

Suppose you sell jewelry and watches. Your customer may have saved for years to buy an item you're not crazy about. You may find yourself disappointed or indifferent to a purchase that seems commonplace. Nonetheless, your customer came to buy what he or she wants and you can't let your opinions influence what your customer regards as important. If your customer wants a watch, you need to present a watch demonstration with as much energy and enthusiasm as you would have used to show off that diamond.

Whether your customer came to buy something boring or exciting, something out of fashion or in the latest style, something outrageously extravagant or inexpensive, keep your opinions to yourself. Listen to your customers and show enthusiasm while you help them select the items that *they* want or need.

Side note: It sometimes seems that the store's buyers were on some sort of drug when they selected the merchandise that hit the floor. However, here is my theory. First, a manufacturer thought it was good enough to make. Second, a buyer agreed and bought it for the store. I figure there has to be a customer out there somewhere who agrees with these other two. It is absolutely my job to find that third person. And until the buyer asks me what to buy for the store, it is my job to sell it—not to have an opinion on it. And frankly, if you want to know what kind of merchandise I like best, it's the merchandise that sells the fastest.

20. Dance According to the Music Played

A great salesperson does not relate to customers in the same rigid way each time, but has the skill to adapt to situations and to the style and tempo of each shopper. You don't need to reinvent yourself every time you are talking with a new customer, nor do you have to develop multiple personalities. Nevertheless, a customer who is doing a foxtrot may not respond very well to a disco beat, and someone who is aggressive may not like a very conservative approach.

I remember teaching a young new salesperson how to open the sale. He watched as I used a very flamboyant approach with a couple in their early 20s. When it was his turn, he used the same approach for a couple in their 60s. No sale. The point is not to qualify your customers, but it's a tremendous benefit to at least look at them and to hear them, to color your presentation in such a way as to make it comfortable for them.

I approached a man one day and asked him how he was doing. He turned on me and said, "You're the third man in a row that's asked me that question." I looked him dead in the eye and said, "Hey buddy. I don't know where else you've been and who else you've talked to, but I'm a nice guy." Then I turned to all of the other salespeople in the store and said, "Right, gang?" They all responded in unison, "He's a nice guy!" The man laughed and eventually bought. Talk about dancing to the music played!

THE FOUR OCCUPATIONS OF THE PROFESSIONAL RETAIL SALESPERSON

Many years ago, I found myself like Walter Mitty (a person who dreamed of doing other jobs), pretending to be several different people while I was on the floor. It was a lot of fun pretending. I found that, as a professional salesperson, I had acted at times like I was in other professions while on the floor. When I aligned myself with these other professionals, I saw a significant change in how successful I could be. Here are four of the occupations I used most often.

The Painter

Truly the only thing that separates your store from others is you. Yeah, you. You know . . . the one who's reading this. And the only thing that separates you from anyone else in retail is your knowledge of your products and people, and the wonderful words you use to show that knowledge and express yourself.

As a painter uses a brush and canvas to create an exhilarating work of art, salespeople use words to create excitement and desire for their products. Whether you are describing the brilliance of a gemstone, the singular advantage of a camera's zoom lens or the style and flash of a particular garment, the words that make up your vocabulary need to paint a picture that will really put a buying twinkle in your customer's eye.

This means that you have to make an accurate assessment of your customers so you can communicate with them in a manner that will make them feel comfortable with you. Customers whose style is Van Gogh may not feel relaxed with a salesperson who is fixated on Picasso.

Painting a word picture of your product requires a thorough knowledge of your products and services. How will you be able to say that your merchandise is durable enough to last a lifetime, or that it's the latest Paris fashion, unless you have taken the time to learn what you need to know about it?

Equally important to your assessment of your customers and your knowledge of your merchandise is your ability to express yourself articulately. Your skill with words will enable you to adapt the product to your client's unique needs and to perform your demonstration in a way that is dynamic, engrossing and exciting to the customer.

Here's an example of a demonstration statement made by a student of mine in a sales class talking about selling shoes and a simple change I made to create excitement. The student said, "These shoes are all leather, which is flexible, making them very comfortable." I changed it to, "You know, when you wear these shoes, you're going to have a smile on your face because one of the great things about these shoes is that they're a soft calfskin leather. And as you wear them, they will mold to the shape of your feet, giving you a custom-made feel. It would be kind of fun to walk around in custom-made shoes, don't you think?"

Remember, a dictionary is vital. And a thesaurus is not a type of dinosaur.

The Architect

Over ten years ago, I developed a logical sequence of steps for making a sale that have served me and hundreds of thousands of other retail professionals all over the world very well. They are affectionately known as the Seven Steps to Success. Don't be fooled by the fact that there are eight listed below. The precheck is an introductory step and hasn't ever been included in my "seven" steps, but it certainly isn't the least important.

- Precheck
- Opening the Sale
- Probing
- The Demonstration
- The Trial Close
- Handling Customer Objections
- Closing the Sale
- Confirmations & Invitations

Each step has a purpose and a goal to be achieved. And as these goals are achieved, you earn the right to move to the next step, and then the next, and then the next. Just as an architect creates a building by starting with the foundation and building up, a logical sequence of steps will turn shoppers into buyers (the subject of the next several chapters). To get the most out of customers, you have to have a plan and follow it, not unlike following a blueprint.

Why does the customer want the product? Is it for personal use or is it a gift? What is the age and gender of the

21

person who will be using it? What will be done with it? Will the item be used conventionally or in some new and unusual way? Or, do you find yourself just demonstrating without the answers to any of these questions?

As the architect of the sale, you want to develop a relationship with your customers and draw out information that will allow your demonstration to turn shoppers into buyers. The reason for gaining this information prior to making a demonstration is to build a solid sale. Without it, you may be missing the point, skipping the logical sequence, or trying to install the ceiling before you have put in the floor.

My favorite example of how not to be an architect is in the beginning of a sales presentation. Let's say you work in a shoe store and you are finishing up with a customer. Another customer comes up to you with a shoe in his hand taken from the shelf, and proceeds to ask if you have the shoe in a size 8 1/2. What would you do at this point? Ninety percent of all retail people would go and see if they had it in stock.

Here is where salespeople break the rule of being an architect and don't do things according to plan. Bringing out the shoe is a demonstration. What happened to opening and probing? Did you say "Hello," or "How are you doing today?" Can you tell me why the customer wants the shoe, or what he will be wearing with it? Were his feet even measured? Clerks go get things on orders from the customers. Professionals build and develop relationships and match merchandise with the customer's desires; they are not there just to step and fetch.

In Opening the Sale, you will learn the value of a person-to-person conversation. This conversation will set the mood for the rest of the presentation. This is mandatory, if you are going to eventually break resistance and develop trust.

The Counselor

I have become a counselor on the selling floor as a result of feeling that every weird, unhappy, deranged and complaining customer wanted only me to help them! Sound familiar?

Counselors get paid lots of money for having clients recline on a couch and tell them their problems as the counselor continues to say three words over and over: "Tell me more." Can you imagine? Two hundred dollars an hour for three words? However, it is an effective technique because it's a non-confrontational way of getting people to tell you about themselves and their needs.

"Tell me more" is useful in eliciting information about a purchase the customer wishes to make. For example, if you can learn more about the customer's underlying need for the item he or she came in to purchase, you may be able to suggest something that will work better than what the buyer originally had in mind.

"Empathy" is a key word in selling today. Using "tell me more" conveys empathy and gives your customers a non-threatening opening to say what's on their minds. It also enables you to see things from the customers' viewpoint. When you are able to stand in their shoes by remembering how *you* feel when *you're* a customer, your patrons will relax and feel better about permitting you to assist them.

"Tell me more" is particularly helpful when a customer comes to return or exchange something. You know the type. The minute these customers get in their car to drive to your store, they start building their story in anticipation of a fight. They slam their car door and start hyperventilating on the way in to see you. You say, "Hello," and off they go. "This thing doesn't work. I hate it. I was sold something I didn't want." And so on. Look them dead in the eye with a sincerely concerned look on your face and say, "You're kidding. Tell me more." I guarantee you they will calm down to a reasonable tone so you can handle the problem. And even if you can't, draw as much anger and frustration out of the customer as you can, then turn the problem over to someone else to handle. It's unlikely the customer will vent anger with such a vengeance all over again.

Since you represent the company, people coming in for the purpose of returning merchandise may be waiting for you to be belligerent. Your skill with the "tell me more" technique may turn a customer predisposed to be angry into one who has positive feelings about you and your store. It also presents you as someone who is representing the customer instead of the store, which in the long run is much better business.

The Showbiz Personality

Have you ever given, or as a customer received, a less than professional presentation? I'll bet you have.

Now, think about how often an entertainer has to do the same show or sing the same song. Tony Bennett, as an example, is a performer who has had a successful career for many decades. His staying power is due in large measure to his talent. However, his long-term success is also the result of his willingness to give a first-class performance every time he performs on stage.

Can you imagine how many times Tony Bennett has sung his hit song, "I Left My Heart In San Francisco"? I would wager that he has sung it during every performance, every year, since making that ultra-famous recording. And he'll continue to do so for the rest of his life. Every time he performs in front of an audience, he'll encounter someone who will be disappointed if he doesn't sing that song.

I remember going to a Neil Diamond concert. (I have all of his albums.) In nearly three hours, he sang 36 hit songs, all of which I knew. But he didn't sing the one song that I was counting on and the evening was a little bit less than I had hoped for because of it.

Do you think that Tony Bennett or other performers enjoy singing the same songs on demand, over and over again? No doubt they'd rather move on to the challenge or diversity of singing new songs, just as you might like to put your older merchandise on the back shelf and demonstrate your new products.

Your customers are entitled to receive a
SHOWTIME PRESENTATION
every single time, period.

It doesn't matter how often you've shown the same item, or how commonplace you think the product is. Your demonstration has to be as fresh and exciting on the hundredth, or the thousandth, time as it was the first time you showed it.

Special note: I feel the "SHOWTIME" spirit is so important that our company, The Friedman Group, had "SHOWTIME" pins made up that every employee must wear at all official functions. And whenever they are asked, "What time is it?" employees must respond "SHOWTIME!" or it personally costs them $25.00. If you don't believe me, ask me or any employee of our company what time it is, and if we don't respond with "SHOWTIME!"—you'll have a check on its way that day (you can't ever count on anybody having cash!).

THE DAILY PRECHECK

- Has a customer ever asked you for an item and you went to get it—only to find it wasn't there?
- How about the customer telling you the item is less expensive down the block and you don't know if it is the same item, or maybe it is less expensive?
- Have you ever been stuck because a price tag has fallen off and you can't give the customer a price?
- How about not having tape in the register or running out of charge slips? Ouch!

These are a few of the hundreds of issues that cause you to lose sales. We are and will continue to be in a world of competitive retailing.

It's difficult enough to make sales,
let alone lose them because of a
lack of information or preparedness.

If the store manager hasn't thought to prepare a checklist to get you ready to sell prior to your shift, then I suggest you do one yourself. Remember—knowledge is power.

There are four general categories of things you can do to really enhance your bid to be successful. Working on these every day may make the difference between success and failure.

How Knowing Prices By Memory Will Benefit You

You're on the floor talking to a shopper, and just when the conversation looks like it might be warming up, your customer asks the price of something in your showcase. You don't even have a clue as to what the price *range* is, let alone the specific price, so you have to get into the locked showcase to find out.

Meanwhile, the customer starts to look at something else, or decides he hasn't got enough time to wait for you to fiddle around, or worse—figures you've probably never sold one of these items before since you are obviously unfamiliar with it. When you don't know the price, the probable result is diminished customer interest—even if the price turns out to be a pleasant surprise.

Let's face it—customers can, and often do, go from hot to cold while you search for the key or expend time to get into the showcase to look for the price on your merchandise. You can keep the momentum of the communication going if you know the price without having to look. It's not worth risking the loss of the sale because you have not committed your prices to memory.

Here is a list of other reasons why memorizing prices is so important to you:

1. It enables you to show products in the customer's price range.
2. You're able to switch more easily if you're out of stock in a requested item.
3. It saves a lot of time.
4. It makes you look like the professional your customer expects.
5. It increases your personal confidence.
6. It increases your credibility.
7. You can give quicker and more efficient phone quotes.
8. You can write up a sale if the tag has fallen off.
9. It increases security—you are aware of switched tags.

10. You can bump up the sale more easily.
11. It helps when adding on.
12. You can better spot missed mark-downs, mark-ups or incorrectly priced items
13. It increases customer confidence in you.
14. It lets you know if you are in line with the competition.
15. You can quote payments on financed merchandise.

Number 15 is one of my favorites. When financing is an option, the difference between a $3,000 item and a $3,500 item may only be a few dollars a month. You're no longer selling $500 more, but maybe only $5 more a month. It is essential that salespeople who deal with financing know or be able to calculate payment information rapidly. The less effort you put in to quoting, the less effort it will seem to be for the customer to make the payments.

How Knowing Your Competition Will Benefit You

Learning everything you can about what and who is competing for the consumer's dollars is another way to make yourself ready for successful professional selling.

Never be so bold as to think you don't have any competition. Not only are you being challenged for your customers by people selling the same product, there are also an enormous number of *other* consumer goods in the marketplace that offer competition for the disposable income your customer could be spending in your store.

Many things compete for customers' attention today and the less you know about where people can spend their money, the less of an edge you have in your ability to convince the buyer to purchase *your* product.

Consider these questions:

- What is the competition saying about your company?
- What is the competition selling?
- How do your merchandise or sales policies compare to those of your competition?
- Does the competition offer service and what is the quality of it?

- What is the competition's pricing structure?

- Is the competition offering sale prices for the same or similar merchandise?

With the answers to these questions, you can no handle a customer's questions about these issues. These may be only some of the answers to seek in your particular retail situation. There are also personal reasons for knowing about the competition, such as increased confidence, which can be a tremendous boost to your sales as well.

Visit your competitors' stores. Request their catalogs. Talk to people who have bought from them. Read all of their ads in the newspaper. Accumulating this kind of information is vital to the success of any sales professional, because being aware of what's going on around you puts you in a superior position.

Want some more reasons why knowing your competition will benefit you? Here they are:

1. Customers won't know more than you do about the competition.
2. You become able to switch from products they sell to products you sell.
3. You will know how your promotions stack up (timing, pricing, etc.)
4. You will know what competitors say about your store (never bad-mouth them, however).
5. You can get merchandise and display ideas.
6. You can inform customers of what they will see.
7. You can spot trends in your industry.
8. You will know what brands are carried.
9. You will gain industry expertise.
10. You will know their credit options.
11. You can offer competitive pricing.
12. You will increase your personal confidence.
13. You can get to be the expert your customers expect you to be.
14. You will increase your chances of getting the customer to buy now.

How Product Knowledge Will Benefit You

There has been a long-standing controversy over whether product knowledge is more important than sales knowledge or vice versa. The fact is that you shouldn't be choosing one or the other, but making a commitment to both.

*Professional salespeople have to be proficient with the techniques and strategies of professional selling, and **also** be knowledgeable enough to answer customer's questions about their merchandise with confidence.*

Don't short-change yourself. With diligence, it doesn't take that long to learn what you need to know to answer a customer's questions intelligently. What are the special features of a particular item? How does one piece of merchandise compare to another of similar price or quality? How does your product work? What are the warranty provisions offered by the manufacturer, or special warranty features offered by your company? What special care or maintenance does it require?

Come on, don't you just hate it when you shop in a store and you know more than the salesperson—and you know nothing? Shoppers expect you to be an authority on what you're selling and they appreciate it when you turn out to be the expert they expected when they came in.

Here are several reasons why product knowledge will benefit you if you work on it every day:

1. It makes you the professional your customers expect.
2. It gives you personal confidence.
3. You're able to show pride in the product.
4. You can handle objections more effectively.
5. It saves time.
6. It allows you to switch with confidence.
7. You can determine potential add-ons more efficiently.
8. It allows you to assist customers with preparation or indoctrination.
9. You can offer cleaning or maintenance suggestions.

10. You can inform regular customers of new products and innovations.
11. It allows you to answer technical questions.
12. It elicits trust from the customer and gives you credibility.
13. Your demonstrations will flow more smoothly.
14. You can give custom-made presentations.
15. You can better satisfy the customer's needs or requests.

Take responsibility. If you don't have a system in your store for learning about product knowledge, start asking fellow salespeople, your store manager, the buyers or write to the vendors. Don't let anyone stop you from being the pro you want to be.

How Walking the Store Will Benefit You

Do you remember your first day working at the store? Was it confusing? Did you feel disoriented? Customers would ask you where something was and you felt helpless, hopeless and out of control? These are natural feelings as a result of not having knowledge of the physical store, its inventory, displays and paperwork. After a few weeks, you seemed to get the hang of it and you felt much better.

But the store changes all the time. New merchandise comes and goes and displays change. There is a need to keep up with changes and continue to exert that control over the store.

In most great professions, people do a walk-through prior to "doing their thing." The surgeon checks to see if the scalpels are there and sharp. The plumber rechecks the truck to make sure the tools needed for the job are there. The school teacher makes sure there are enough tests to give out. The singer does a sound check. And on and on. How about you? Showing up for work at 10:00 a.m. when you have to start at 10:00 a.m. won't cut it. It may seem like preaching, but I can tell you how out of sync I have personally felt by not getting to my location early and scoping out my turf.

Here is a list of reasons why walking the store prior to your shift will benefit you:

1. It lets you know when you need to re-stock.
2. You can put misplaced merchandise back in its place.
3. You will be aware of new product arrivals.
4. You can quickly find appropriate merchandise for customers.
5. You can spot needed housekeeping or maintenance problems.
6. You can correct in-store signage.
7. You will know what items have been marked down or moved.
8. You will know how many "hot items" are left in stock.
9. You can prioritize things that need to be done that day.
10. You can spot the need for display changes or shifts.
11. You can find out about new in-store promotions and media advertisements.
12. You can find and match up mis-matched items.
13. You will be aware of potential or actual theft problems.
14. You can take care of lighting needs (lights out, misdirected spots, etc.).
15. You're ready to do business (paperwork and register supplies stocked).

There is No Substitute for Preparation

The skills you need to succeed as a professional retail salesperson, like the skills needed to become a successful doctor, lawyer or plumber, can be mastered through the commitment of time, energy and effort.

The key to success is organization and preparation, for which there is no substitute. Preparation means:

Performing a daily precheck, tasks designed to organize you every day on the selling floor, and make you more confident and knowledgeable.

Your success depends entirely on your communication skills, your knowledge and your enthusiasm.

When you are prepared,
you'll know what you're on the floor to do:
SELL
You'll know the best time to do it:
NOW
And you'll know exactly what time it is:
SHOWTIME!

HOT TIPS AND KEY INSIGHTS

- Your success as a salesperson depends entirely on *your* ability to open up to customers, to communicate with them and to satisfy their needs.

- Too many salespeople are professionals who often act like clerks. They do an adequate job of executing routine tasks at work, but they don't develop special skills, "go the extra mile," do their homework or cultivate their clients.

- Selling today is remarkably different than it has been in the past for two major reasons: people tend to be cautious about where they spend their money and there are more consumer goods than ever, which fosters more competition for the customer's disposable income.

- The secret ingredients to success as a professional salesperson can be summed up in three words: preparation, preparation, preparation.

- In retail selling, performing painstaking "precheck" chores lays the groundwork for your success on the floor.

- There are 10 *daily* elements to the precheck: satisfying every single customer, keeping personal problems outside the store, avoiding congregating on the selling floor, acknowledging every customer's presence, never qualifying a customer by appearance, respecting the customer's "space," not interrupting the customer, always looking professional, showing the merchandise whether you like it or not, and dancing to the music played.

- *Long-range* precheck activities involve the commitment of a larger amount of time and energy, and may have to be done after work and on your days off.

- *Long-term* precheck activities include increasing your product knowledge, learning product prices by memory, knowing your competition, and continually walking the store.

- A great salesperson does not relate to customers in the same way each time, but has the skill to adapt to situations and to the style and tempo of each shopper, acting as painter, architect, counselor and show-business personality.

- Getting out on the floor every day and interacting with customers build your confidence. On a slow day, use the time you have to enhance your capabilities for when things pick up again.

- When you are prepared, you never lose sight of what you came to do today—sell; the best time to sell—now; and exactly what time it is—**SHOWTIME!**

CHAPTER TWO

OPENING THE SALE

The most critical step in selling may very well be your opening line.

I have heard and read little on the subject of opening the sale. It seems like every lecture or book on selling talks about closing or objections and glosses over what I feel is the major downfall in retail selling — opening the sale.

Opening the sale encompasses two major components: art and science. The science part consists of the things we absolutely know about opening the sale from experience, and the art is your personal ability to make the rules work with your own personality. A plastic surgeon can fix your nose (science), but there is no guarantee that it will look good (art). Let's first take a look at some of the facts we know about opening the sale.

People Behave Reactively

When you have had a very bad experience in your life, it is stored in your mind. When something happens to remind you of that bad experience, you may react without ever being aware of what you are doing.† Here are some examples of how that might apply:

1. A little girl falls off a horse when she is 4 years old. She is now 30 and doesn't want to go horseback riding with her friends.
2. I buy a Ford car when I'm 16. I spend a lot of money fixing it up. I have trouble making payments. I am now 35 and I go to look at cars. Not Fords.
3. My mother forces me to finish my dinner when I am young. The meal happens to be fish. I won't eat fish now.
4. I dive into a pool head-first. I hit my head on the bottom of the pool. It's five years later, and I still don't dive into pools.
5. I go into a retail store looking for a special suit for a very important occasion. The salesperson is weak on product knowledge and is very pushy and aggressive. I don't like retail salespeople any more.
6. I shop for insurance. The salesperson seems to give me good advice. I check with a friend and find out the salesperson did not give me the best advice. I now distrust retail salespeople. (This is not a mistake— think about it.)

There are some very good scientific expressions that support this entire theory:

For every cause there is an effect.
For every action there is an opposite and equal reaction.
And for every stimulus there is a response.

This all relates very well to opening the sale.

Causing a Negative Reaction From the Beginning

The game is to avoid stimulating a negative response from your customers. I have asked this question in thousands of lectures and seminars on selling: "How many of

†Hubbard, L. Ron. Dianetics, The Modern Science of Mental Health. Los Angeles: Bridge Publications, 1950.

you have had a bad experience with a salesperson and how many of you generally don't like salespeople?" Every hand goes up, every time. People do not like salespeople. (Doesn't it make you feel good to know people don't like you and they don't even know you?). Here are some of the reasons salespeople are not liked:

1. Customers couldn't find one when they really needed one.
2. The salesperson sold them something they didn't need or sold them the wrong product.
3. The salesperson was too slick or pushy.
4. The salesperson didn't know enough about the merchandise.
5. The customer needed more time to make a decision and the salesperson kept pushing for the sale.
6. The salesperson was indifferent to the customer as a person.

It's a shame, but all of these examples are true and evident every day in the world of retail selling. You don't need to be qualified or have a license to get on the floor and bring havoc to the lives of people. And because these things are true, it makes opening the sale that much more difficult. Your job now becomes one to get past all of that resistance so you have an opportunity to develop a relationship and make a sale.

The Primary Goal of Opening the Sale is to Get Past Resistance

What happens when a salesperson greets a customer when negative feelings about salespeople are stored in the customer's mind? Do you think you can predict the response in 90 percent of all these contacts? You bet you can: it's "No thanks, I'm just looking." It's amazing how many salespeople hear this and never seem to figure out how to get beyond that reply. I'm not talking about how to handle it once you've heard it—I mean how to avoid getting such a response to begin with. I was in a store recently where the salesperson said, "Are you looking for anything in particular, or are you just looking?" Talk about sleeping on the job! I had the irresistible desire to smack him across the face and tell him to wake up!

Establish a Person-to-Person Relationship Rather Than a Salesperson-to-Customer Relationship

A person-to-person relationship is the opposite of what I refer to as "clerking." Think of the last time you were in a store. Can you remember the kind of relationship you had with the salesperson? Or how about doing this exercise: Write down the stores and the salespeople you can name that you go back to time and time again because of the personal relationship and the terrific service.

This entire process begins in the opening of the sale. Take the few extra seconds in the beginning and you will have a customer who not only enjoys the process, but might spend a lot more money.

OPENING LINES

If you greet a customer with a business line, then you will get a reactive and resistant response such as, "I'm just looking," or something similar. What is more amazing is that most of the time customers don't even know they are saying it. It's a spontaneous reaction—but customers also know that it works. It sends salespeople away—thank you very much.

I'm sure you will agree it would be nice if we could go up to customers and be helpful and say, "What can I do for you?" or "How can I be of assistance?" Well folks, here is the truth. It does work . . . with three out of ten customers who know what they want, or with people who go to McDonalds. But not if you want to sell to the majority of the people you talk to in a retail store, where people really don't need what you have. Therefore, rule number one in creating an opening dialogue would be:

Opening Lines Must Have Nothing To Do With Business

You really shouldn't go any further in this book until you understand that your opening salutation cannot be about business. It's as if you had a neon sign over your head that reads, "Don't trust me, I'm a salesperson." If your opening cannot be business related to be effective, then it holds true that the most used and written-about technique, the "merchandise approach," would also be ineffective.

The Merchandise Approach is Ineffective and Rude

My brother calls me on the phone and tells me that he has just purchased a $500 tennis racquet. I think, "That's reasonable—for someone who's nuts." I don't like tennis, and I find what he is telling me a little difficult to understand—particularly since he isn't that great a tennis player. I am, however, a scuba diver and I need a new mask and snorkel. As I enter the sporting goods store all excited about getting a new mask, what should be on display at the front of the store? You've got it—tennis racquets. I stop and pick up—guess which one? You've got it again. The $500 racquet just like the one my brother purchased. As I'm looking to see if it has a motor or some built-in parts to help his game, out of nowhere a salesperson comes over and says, "It just came in, isn't it a beauty? I'm sure that no matter how well you play now, it will help improve your game." Any guesses about what I'm thinking? *"Get off my back, you idiot. I don't want a racquet."*

A very talented salesperson in a Florida jewelry store told me about the first time she was on the selling floor. She had just been promoted to the floor from a clerical job. She eyed a customer coming in and started the long journey of making her first presentation. The customer had his head buried in a ring showcase in the front of the store. She walked over and started the conversation by saying, "I see that you are interested in our beautiful rings." His simple reply? "No, I'm the carpenter and I was told the case needed repair."

First off, how could you possibly determine what customers want or why they have come in by what catches their eye, or where they just happen to stop? Second, it's rude to have someone come into your store, where you spend a major portion of your life, and not even say

"Hello" before you start your sales presentation. The merchandise approach is lazy and can ruin more relationships than it helps.

However, if you are inclined to sell only two or three out of the ten people that come in, use it because there will always be two or three who know what they want and won't let even you deter them—no matter how hard you try to mess things up.

So, here are the five worst opening lines in selling:

1. Can I help you? (How may I help you?)
2. Are you looking for anything in particular?
3. Can I answer any of your questions?
4. Do you know about our sale?
5. We just got that in. It's really great, isn't it?

From reading the customer service points in the previous chapter, you know the importance of getting your customers to open up and talk. Therefore, rule number two in opening the sale would have to be:

Opening Lines Should be Questions to Encourage Conversation

Person-to-person conversations are the key ingredient in the process of breaking down resistance. Short and quick statements do not get you anywhere. Have some fun. Make your questions interesting. But don't forget to make your initial greeting a question.

It must have been 15 years or so ago that a lady came into the store with a child in a stroller. You might think I would have said, "What a beautiful little baby?" Sound good? No way. It's not a question and doesn't get you past the resistance that may be there. This is what I did say. "That's a beautiful little baby. Where did you get it?" Now I know you might be laughing, but the truth is that I used the line then and have been using it ever since. It has never, ever failed to get a terrific response.

It's not a requirement, but it's also a good idea to keep your questions as open as possible as opposed to closed questions that encourage a yes or no response. Try using who, what, where, when, why or how.

A closed question:

Salesperson: Is it still busy in the mall?

Customer: No.

An open question:

Salesperson: How's the traffic in the mall?

Customer: Well, when I got here this afternoon it was like a zoo, but it's started to thin out a little and . . .

Have you ever wondered why a customer says "I'm just looking," after asking them, "How's the weather outside?" Simply put, common, expected and uninteresting opening lines by salespeople aren't enough to cause a personal conversation. Therefore, the third rule in opening lines must be:

Opening Lines Should Be Unique, Sincere, or Different Enough to Cause a Conversation

This is the hard part. This completely separates the clerks from the professionals. All over the world I have trouble getting this across. I hope I can now with this explanation.

People find shopping to be either entertainment or one big pain in the neck. People are generally not indifferent to going into retail stores. Wouldn't it be fun if you could create an environment where your customers had a great time and would spend lots of money? I believe you are in control of how the entire presentation goes. And it all starts with the quality of your opening line.

If the process of getting into a conversation with a customer were easy, everyone would be doing it and there would be no need for this type of information. People find it difficult at best. In fact, people find it almost impossible. It's partly because they don't want to put in the time that's necessary to do the job. And it also seems that salespeople forget to act the way they do outside of work. You can't be successful being one kind of person in life and another kind of person on the sales floor.

In Rule #2, I talked about using a question to encourage conversation. The third rule is to be unique, sincere and different. Although these are pretty good guidelines, I could never give you "your" opening lines. Opening lines are to retail selling what fingerprints are to your personal uniqueness.

My style happens to be humor. I have a lot of years under my belt telling everyone I meet a joke, or trying in everyday conversation to make people laugh. Marlene Cordry, a vice president for The Friedman Group, also worked for me in retail many years ago. Her style is, "I'll get you because the look on my face is so helpful and non-aggressive that you can't resist letting me talk to you." Everyone is different, and just like a singer, you have to develop a style that suits you and you can be comfortable with. At the end of this chapter you will find 42 opening lines. All of these lines have been used and have worked. The only reason I don't put a guarantee on them is that you are the only one that can bring them to life.

OPENING MOVES

The secret word in opening the sale is "schmoozing." I'm not sure, but I think the word "schmoozing" is Irish! It means "small talk." But don't think just because it's SMALL talk, that it's small in importance. The whole concept of breaking down resistance and establishing a relationship with your customers is best described as schmoozing. Throughout the remainder of the book, when I refer to schmoozing, I'm really referring to the use of all three rules for opening lines as stated (non-business related, questions, and unique). And don't forget, you can't lose when you schmooze.

Please do not by-pass this information as another chapter to briefly read. It IS important. The quality of your opening dialogue with your customer is everything at the beginning of your presentation. Of course, if it isn't good, you really don't have to worry about the rest of your presentation because you either won't have a customer to talk to or you may find yourself rushed, or heaven forbid, completely out of control.

Opening the Sale is as Physical as it is Verbal

Have you ever walked near a customer without even mumbling a word, and still heard, "I'm just looking." You think to yourself, "What did I do?" The point of customer-to-salesperson resistance is proven again.

Or how about this: You're working on a display and there are two or three other salespeople in the store. Who does the customer come to? You, of course. Why? Because you are busy and don't appear able to be pushy or aggressive. Customers feel they can interrupt you, get their question answered and move on unharmed.

Violating Customers' Perceived Personal Space

People need and want personal shopping freedom. The way you approach the customer can be seen by the customer as a violation of that space. As you approach customers, three things may happen:

1. The customer goes off in another direction to avoid the contact.
2. The customer gives you a reactive line such as "I'm just looking" before you even say a word.
3. The customer tells you what he or she wants or asks you a question.

The space in front of customers is perceived as theirs, so any approach in that space is a violation. You can cross it and say your hellos or you can walk parallel to customers and say your hellos. Just try to stay out of their direct path. Of course, you may think I'm nuts, and I am. But after practicing this technique, you will also be a believer.

The 180 Degree Pass-By

Upon making your approach, you should have something in your hand. This gives the customers the impression that you have something on your mind other than slamming them up against the wall and taking all of their money. Looking busy has always been a key strategy in opening the sale.

The 180 degree pass-by is the best technique I have ever developed to open the sale. It merely involves walking near the customer, saying "Hello," or "How are you," and walking past them. Then, after taking three or four steps, turn around at a safe distance and with a quizzical look on your face, say something like, "May I ask you a question?" Most of the time, the customer will turn around, take a few steps TOWARD YOU and say, "Sure." Of course, the big problem is: what's the question? Here's where you're on your own. I couldn't possibly give you an opening line that fits you and your style exactly. What works for me might not work for you. For those of you who are not as creative as you'd like to be or have difficulty coming up with opening lines, don't despair. In the back of this chapter you will find 42 of them that you can steal.

Let's Review a Little:

You spot a customer coming into the store. You put something in your hand and start the approach, walking parallel to the customer. You have a huge smile on your face and as you get near you say, "Hello," or "How are you?" You wait for a reply as you continue to walk and pass them by. You make the turn and say, "May I ask you a question?" The customer responds "Sure," and you say something like, "I can tell by the number of packages you have that there must be some great bargains out there. What am I missing by being locked up in the store today?" The customer will generally respond with comfortable conversation.
For example:

Salesperson: I can tell by the number of packages you have that there must be some great bargains out there. What am I missing by being locked up in the store today?

Customer: Nothing really. I just had to pick up some gifts for a party we're going to.

44

The big decision now is whether to get right in to business or keep schmoozing? You guessed right! Keep on schmoozing. The extra 30 seconds you spend in schmoozing will result in watching the pain, resistance and terror drain out of the customer's face as you develop a relationship.

Salesperson: A party! That really sounds like a lot of fun. Wouldn't it be even more fun if the party was for you?

The Process of Hanging Out

Any time you have the opportunity to hang out in a non-business conversation with your customers, take it. They want it. It makes them feel special. And it's fun. People like it when other people take an interest in them personally. Nobody wants to be treated as if he or she were a number or just another customer.

Here are some more examples with the potential of hanging out:

Salesperson: I saw you early this morning when the mall first opened! How long have you been shopping?

Customer: All day! I have relatives coming in from out of town for a visit and I want everything to be just right.

Salesperson: Oh relatives! That always makes for a busy schedule. When do they arrive? . . . (and on and on.)

Salesperson: That's an enormous box of cookies! Who are they for?

Customer: I have a daughter in college who I send care packages to.

Salesperson: Great! You know, I always looked forward to those brown paper packages from home. What school is she attending? . . . (and on and on.)

Salesperson: So it looks like the whole family is along

45

today! What are you all up to?

Customer: We're power shopping! We just closed on a brand new house and wanted to start decorating it right away.

Salesperson: How exciting! It's been a lifetime dream of mine to buy a house. What area did you decide to buy in? . . . (and on and on.)

Salesperson: Have you had a chance to make it to the polls this morning?

Customer: No, I've been shopping all morning for some different earrings. I just got my hair cut short last week and all of my old ones look funny.

Salesperson: A haircut! Looks great! What made you decide to cut your hair? . . . (and on and on.)

GETTING INTO BUSINESS: THE TRANSITION

After a few moments of person-to-person conversation, it's time to get down to business and move into probing. After all of the experimenting and research I have done, I keep coming up with the same transition question:

"What brings you into our store today?"

That does the job beautifully. Variations such as "What brings you into Harry's?" or even "What brings you in?" are also workable. This question is superb as it is not only open-ended, but is as broad a question as you can get to open people up. Since you want your customers to communicate and tell you things, lines like "Are you looking for anything in particular?" or "Are you looking for (item)?" could never be as effective.

If after schmoozing you use the transition question, "What brings you into our store today?" and still get a resistant response, such as "I'm just looking," now what?

Shoppers are smart. They know exactly how to get a salesperson to leave them alone. They're very practiced at it. With a quick resistant line and a stern facial expression, customers can get any salesperson to walk away. What's the line? "I'm just looking," of course. Here are the top five conversation busters of all time.

1. I'm just looking.
2. I'm just browsing.
3. I just wanted to see what you have.
4. I'm just killing time.
5. My husband (or wife) is next door shopping.

At this point in your presentation, you really have to take a look at what is happening. You have done the pass-by, you have schmoozed, you have used the transition question and you are still getting this reaction? Yes, and it's common. The customers probably don't even realize they're saying it. It is a defensive shield that has become a workable solution and automatic reaction to the queries of salespeople. It really hit home one day when Marlene Cordry and I were touring stores in a mall together. As a salesperson approached her, she said, "I'm just on my lunch break." I asked her why she said that and she said, "Said what?" She then told me it was the excuse she had used when she worked in a mall, and it worked so well that it became a habit.

Salespeople who are trying to salvage the presentation at this point may make another error in trying to be helpful. As a response to the defensive shields given by customers, salespeople often say the following:

- Just let me know if you have any questions, I'll be over there.
- My name is Harry if you have any questions.

Here's how the customer hears what you just said:

My name is Harry, the SALESPERSON, and I'll be right over here where SALESPEOPLE stand, in case you have any questions for a SALESPERSON who only wants to SELL you something you don't want.

Let's face it, the customers put up defensive shields because they don't like salespeople. The solution to those defensive shields couldn't possibly be to remind them to hate you more. There is a better way.

The Take-Away

The take-away is a technique used to defuse the defensive shields used by your customers. It involves two parts.

1. Agreement that it is okay to look.
2. An exact repeating of the customer's defensive shield phrased as a question.

Here's the take-away handling each of the top five defensive shields:

Transition:	What brings you into our store today?
Defensive Shield:	I'm just looking.
Agreement:	That sounds like fun.
Take-away:	What are you looking for?
Transition:	What brings you into our store today?
Defensive Shield:	I'm just browsing.
Agreement:	I love to browse, too.
Take-away:	What are you browsing for?
Transition:	What brings you into our store today?
Defensive Shield:	I just wanted to see what you have.
Agreement:	Well, great!
Take-away:	What kinds of things would you like us to have? (Put a big smile on your face for this one!)
Transition:	What brings you into our store today?
Defensive Shield:	I'm just killing time.
Agreement:	We all need a little more time to kill.
Take-away:	What are you looking for while you're killing time?
Transition:	What brings you into our store today?
Defensive Shield:	My husband's just next door shopping.

Agreement:	So you're on your own for a while.
Take-away:	What are you looking for while he's shopping?

You are going to be so delighted with how effective this technique is! In the majority of cases, your customer will open up and off you go into probing. However, I must caution you that "What brings you into our store today?" is a probing question, and works best after schmoozing as a transition question. When used as an opening line, it becomes "Can I help you," and the take-away very rarely works.

If after you have schmoozed and used the take-away you hear, "I'm just looking," for the second time, there are only a couple of things you can do at this point. One is to turn over the sale to another salesperson or, if you really have the spirit, the Fun Take-Away.

The Turnover

It's a fact of life, some customers will have a problem with how you look, talk, act, your color, height, weight or the fact that you remind them of their dreaded Uncle Louie or Aunt Alice. These are all things out of your control. After the second, "I'm just looking," you should merely say, "Enjoy!" and walk away. Choose another salesperson who looks completely different than you and have them re-approach the shopper.

The Fun Take-Away

I hate to lose an opportunity to sell, so I have developed a few ideas for times when I hear "I'm just looking" a second time.

When I ask, "What brings you into our store today," and they say, "I'm just looking," I use the take-away. "That's terrific! What are you looking for?" The customer says, "I'm just looking." Then I take them over to an item that has a price tag with "I'm just looking" printed on it and a reduced price. I say, "Aren't you lucky! It's on sale today!" Or sometimes I walk them right over to a printed sign that says, "As of March 1, 1992, it is now legal to look."

Another one of my favorite memories of "breaking the mold" was while working in a client's jewelry store. I was "up" when an older lady walked through the door. No doubt you've seen someone just like her. She had blue hair and one of those animal shoulder wraps with the head still attached! By my estimation she'd been drinking for two or three weeks straight. I was at a loss for an opening line. What do you say to her? Then it hit me, I walked right up to her and asked, "So what do you want to do now?" She replied, "Dance!" I grabbed her and we proceeded to waltz around the store while I hummed. She was a sweet old lady who happened to love the attention. My next move was something I can only get away with when dancing with drunk, blue-haired ladies. I asked, "What do you need to make you even more beautiful than you are now?" "Earrings," was her answer.

I tangoed with her over to the case with our most expensive pearl studs, about $500. I brought them out of the case and urged her to try them on. "But that's against the law, you can't try on pierced earrings," she said, concerned. The truth is that it isn't against the law and never was. Retail salespeople have just been too lazy to allow their customers to do so. All that's required is cleaning them with alcohol afterwards, for health reasons. I could have told my blue-haired lady that, but I wanted to make her stay with us more exciting, so I whispered, "I know, let's break the law!"

I ended up selling her the $500 earrings and she left feeling quite special. The postscript to the whole story is that she happened to be on a tour bus with 50 more drunk, blue-haired ladies. We made our year that day.

This lighthearted approach is a lot of fun, but I caution you: if you don't think you can do it, don't. Turning it over to another salesperson will be just fine.

Once You Get Customers Talking

People are more comfortable when they are talking to other people who seem genuinely interested in what they have to say. It is far more important for you to get customers talking than it is for you to carry the conversation.

The more customers speak with you, the more they begin to feel comfortable with you as a person, not a salesperson. Recall the last party you attended and anybody you met at the party for the first time. Chances are the people you liked the best among your new acquaintances were those who asked you questions and seemed to care about what you had to say. Your customers will be no different.

Personalizing Your Remarks

There are several different signals to watch for to help you personalize your remarks:

Children:
Whenever customers come in with children, you have an obvious subject for conversation. What parent doesn't love to talk about his or her children? Don't just comment on how cute kids are, but find out how old they are, if they're always this good natured and if they sleep through the night.

Comment on how well the child speaks, how much he or she can do, how functional the stroller is that the parent is using. A word of warning: Be careful not to guess a baby's gender; the odds are that you will be wrong half the time.

Personalized Clothing:
If people come in wearing college or professional team shirts, ask if they went to that school, what the campus is like, did they watch the game last night, or what they think of the team this year. Do *not* express your opinion about the school or the team. As my grandmother used to say, "dance according to the music" the customer is playing.

Cars:
If you are within sight of customers as they drive up, whether their cars are new, old, unusual or expensive, feel free to talk about them. We all have some pride in our automobile. Whatever the car, most customers will be receptive to talking about it.

51

Current Events:
Are exciting or tumultuous things happening in the world that most people know about? Use the latest crisis, space probe, visit from a foreign dignitary, or geological event such as a volcanic eruption or earthquake in your opening line. When choosing a current event though, make sure that it is not too controversial. With some customers, bringing up a scandal about the mayor or another political figure may prove to be risky.

Holidays:
Most people make plans during the holidays, whether it's a three-day vacation, a dinner with relatives or just rest and relaxation at home. If a holiday is approaching, ask customers what their plans are. If the holiday just ended, ask if they did anything special.

What If You Have No Clue?

Often people walk into your store who do not immediately present you with an idea to start up a conversation. To avoid having no opening line, prepare some general topics which have universal appeal. The more opening lines you have in your back pocket ready for use, the better.

One Hundred of Your Own

You should sit down and write at least 100 of your own opening lines. In case you have trouble getting started, I've provided a list of opening lines below. This list is best used as a take-off point. No one can come up with your opening lines. You have to develop your own. They have to be *by* you, because you may not be comfortable saying what someone else would.

1. We're thinking about putting down new carpet; which sample do you like?
2. (Walking by with several small boxes in your hand) Could you do me a favor? Could you push that top box back a little? You know, when one falls they all fall!

3. Boy, I'm starving for a new joke. What's your favorite one?
4. I'd like to take my wife out for a great fish dinner. Do you have any recommendations?
5. I noticed your daughter has her ears pierced. My little girl is about her age. How did she react?
6. I see you're wearing a tour jacket. Did you go to that concert last night?
7. May I ask you a question? Do you think women prefer candy or flowers on Valentine's day?
8. I noticed you walking out of the hair salon across the way. Who do you use over there?
9. It looks pretty hot out there today. Would you like something cold to drink?
10. It looks like those bags are heavy! Would you like me to hold them while you look around?
11. I couldn't help but overhear you and your friend talking about that new movie. I was planning on seeing it. How is it?
12. Could you do me a favor? My mother wants a picture of her boy hard at work. Could you take a picture of me over by the counter?
13. Do you have an update on the game?
14. I noticed your shoes. Do they really give more support?
15. I just bought some fresh coloring books! Would your kids like to break them in?
16. What do you think of this hat on me?
17. I'm planning my vacation today. Where have you been that's exciting?
18. Your little boy talks so well! Is he going to school yet?
19. What a great haircut! Where do you have it done?
20. So, how is the high school doing in basketball this year?
21. I see you're driving a Honda. How does it perform?
22. Did you have a chance to see the activities in the center court?
23. Aren't you glad the weather man was wrong today?
24. Well, it's almost tax day. Are you the early bird or do you mail yours off at the last minute?

25. Twins! Double trouble, double fun! How old are they?
26. How did you celebrate yesterday's holiday?
27. What a great outfit! How long do you suppose it took to sew all of those sequins on?
28. Your hair looks beautiful french-braided. How long does it take you?
29. Some little person has been to McDonalds today! Were your kids born wanting McDonalds, too? Mine were.
30. Can you believe we've been so long without rain? Have you started the water conservation mandate?
31. I see you're wearing a Laker's shirt. Do you think they'll make the play-offs?
32. I've been stuck in the store all day. What's the news on the space shuttle?
33. This is a three-day weekend, isn't it? How's the traffic out there?
34. What a great tan! Are you lucky enough to always look that way or have you just returned from vacation?
35. The lottery is up to $62 million. Have you bought your ticket yet?
36. Did you see the Grammys last night?
37. Wow, are those brand-new skis? Where are you going to use them first?
38. You really loaded up at the book store. What books did you buy?
39. Can I ask your opinion? The buyer just ordered this model; do you think we should order this other model, too?
40. Look at that cast! What happened to your arm?
41. Six kids! Do these all belong to you?
42. We've been having a little discussion. When do you think we should put our holiday decorations up here at the store?

WORKING TWO CUSTOMERS AT ONCE

What happens when there are more customers than salespeople? In many retail selling situations, particularly with small, high-priced items such as jewelry, security measures must be taken into consideration. You should not physically wait on two customers at once in those situations.

Suppose, however, that you are working with Customer A and Customer B enters the store. You have to acknowledge Customer B. If you don't, he may leave without anyone saying hello. This represents a loss in potential business and is rude. Yet, your allegiance is to Customer A.

The Verbal Contract

How do you excuse yourself without angering Customer A? With a lot of love and care. You ask Customer A, "Would you do me a favor," to which they always reply, "Yes."

"Can you hang on for just a moment while I say hello to that customer? I'll be right back. Will that be okay?"

You will actually hear Customer A say "Yes." In a sense, Customer A has *contracted* with you to stay put.

Now, you walk over to Customer B and say, "How are you doing? Can you do me a favor?" This greeting serves both as your opening line and sets up Customer B for a verbal contract. He'll give you a perplexed look and be thinking, "I don't know if I want to do you a favor, I just walked into the store." Incredibly, however, the customer always says "Okay."

You then say, "Can you hang on for just a minute? I'm finishing with that customer over there and then I'll be right with you. Will that be okay?" If Customer B says, "Yes," which happens frequently, then he's made a verbal contract with you. He won't leave. He'll stay in the store because he told you he would.

Understandably, some customers will say, "No, I've got to get going," or "I'm going next door and I'll check back, later," or the like. But most will say, "Yes."

When attempting to handle two customers, using the verbal contract yields far greater results than what usually happens in retail selling: The salesperson is serving Customer A. Customer B enters the store. The salesperson turns around to Customer B and says, "I'll be right with you," then he turns back to Customer A and soon after learns that Customer B has departed.

For review, let's walk through a Verbal Contract scenario:

Salesperson: We just need your bank information, right here.

Customer A: I always hate filling out these forms.

Salesperson: Oh, I know what you mean. (Spots Customer B.) Could you excuse me for just a minute? I want to let this gentleman know that I'll be with him shortly. Is that all right?

Customer A: Sure.

Salesperson: Thanks. (Approaches Customer B.) Hi, could you do me a favor? I'm finishing up with that lady right now and I will be with you in just a minute. Is that all right?

Customer B: Okay.

Salesperson: Thanks. (Returns to Customer A.) Just your signature right here would be fine.

Here's another:

Customer A: I think my sister will really enjoy this table cloth for her party.

Salesperson: From what you've told me, I know it will be perfect. Say, could you excuse me for one second? I want to let that young lady know I'll be with her as soon as you and I are through. Is that all right?

Customer A: Sure.

Salesperson: Thanks. (Walking over to customer B.) Hello there! Could you do me a favor? I'm just finishing up with that lady over there, and I will be with you in just a few moments. Will that be all right?

Customer B: Okay.

Salesperson: Thank you. (Returning to customer A.) Let me just take your driver's license number down on this check and you'll be on your way to that party!

The verbal contract works because you are asking people to grant you a small favor using great courtesy. I'll bet you can achieve a favorable outcome the first time you use it.

HOW HAVE YOU BEEN OPENING?

Opening the sale may be the most important part of the selling process and is the key to what transpires throughout the rest of your presentation. By effectively opening the sale, you can reduce resistance and enhance your ability to ask probing questions. Ask yourself how effective you have been in this area previously and have you given it enough thought?

How perky, interesting and clever have your opening lines been? Have you built a rapport with customers on a person-to-person basis? From kids to adults, men and women, to couples and groups, have you worked on effectively opening the sale? If you'll take the time to write down 75 to 100 opening lines and practice them, you'll be at the cash register more than you have ever been before.

HOT TIPS AND KEY INSIGHTS

- To effectively open the sale, start with a great opening line, and avoid the trite, such as "May I help you?"
- The percentage of customers who are really "just looking" is so small that, as a rule of thumb, it makes sense never to believe any customer is "just looking."
- The Merchandise Approach, which involves greeting customers by commenting on the particular item they first looked at upon entering the store, originally was brilliant because it allowed the salesperson to demonstrate items to customers almost immediately. Today, it is outmoded and ineffective.
- Your goal is to avoid salesperson-to-customer relationships and instead develop *person-to-person* relationships, which pay off remarkably better.

- The two keys to effectively opening the sale are to:
  (1) Break down the innate resistance that customers have towards salespeople, and
  (2) Develop a person-to-person, not a salesperson-to-customer, relationship.
- Realistically, if you introduce yourself as a salesperson you risk encountering negative reactions from customers. It is mandatory that you *avoid behavior that traditionally has resulted in negative reactions among customers.*
- Effective opening lines have nothing to do with business and are best if posed as innovative, unusual or clever questions to encourage conversation.
- Avoid asking questions that can be answered by a single word such as *yes* or *no*, because your chance of building any rapport from the exchange is slim.
- If you tend to rush through the opening, slow down; the merchandise isn't going anywhere and neither are the customers. There is no room today for clerks who ask mundane questions or hurry through opening the sale, thereby generating a fraction of the sales achievable had they taken the time to develop some effective opening lines.
- If you use compliments, do so very carefully, as they can backfire on you. If you compliment someone on his or her clothing, make sure it's something spectacular or unusual.
- People are more comfortable when they are talking to others who seem genuinely interested in what they have to say. It is far more important for you to get customers talking than it is for you to carry the conversation.
- Use all available clues to personalize your remarks to each customer, noting the customer's children or vehicle, for example, or current events and holidays.
- No one can come up with your opening lines; you have to develop your own. They have to be *by* and *of* you, because you may not be comfortable saying what someone else uses. Devote as many hours to practicing openings as you do to learn about your products.

- To overcome customers' resistance to being approached directly, focus on how you can proceed in a friendlier, less threatening way. Assume that customers don't want you to come too close to their personal space, and avoid walking directly at someone. Instead use the 180 Degree Pass-By.

- Customers are drawn to the busy salesperson because they perceive that there will be no pressure, or they can get a quick answer to their questions. So act busy.

- The most effective method for moving from opening the sale to probing is to use a broad-based transition question that makes customers actually tell you why they're in the store, such as "What brings you into our store today?"

- To know if a customer is really just looking, you can apply the "Take-Away." When a customer says, "...just looking," exclaim something like: "Terrific. What were you looking for?" which takes away the shield.

- It's critical to spend an appropriate amount of time building rapport through "schmoozing." Simply walking up to customers and saying, "What brings you in today?" doesn't break through their resistance.

- If you've gone through all the steps and still get a second, "Just looking. . ." turn the sale over to another salesperson. Someone else may be able to get that customer to open up—it's not your fault and there are other customers.

- Use the Verbal Contract to serve two customers: Ask Customer A, "Would you do me a favor?" to which the answer is always, "Yes." "Can you hang on for just a moment while I say hello to that customer? I'll be right back. Will that be okay?" You will actually hear Customer A say, "Yes." Customer A has *contracted* with you to stay put.

- Opening the sale is the most important part of the process and is the key to what transpires throughout the rest of the selling process. By effectively opening the sale, you can reduce resistance and enhance your ability to ask probing questions.

- If you will take the time to write down 75 to 100 opening lines and practice them, you'll be at the cash register more than you have ever been before.

CHAPTER THREE
PROBING

Most salespeople can find out what the customer wants. It takes a professional to find out the personal motivation the customer has for wanting it in the first place.

By now you should be committed to working out your opening lines to the point where you feel confident and comfortable using them with customers. While opening the sale is an important step that needs to be rehearsed as often as possible, it still doesn't guarantee you the final sale . . . and the earnings you would like.

You may learn what your customers *want* through your opening discussions, but you still may not know *why* they desire to purchase a particular item. Is it for a special occasion, or for a valued employee? Or could it be an item they want for themselves? More often than not, the sale is more complicated than simply determining what a customer wants.

Opening As Many Doors As Possible

By developing the ability to *probe* and discover why a customer wants a particular item, you can greatly enhance your opportunity to assist that customer. By skillfully determining the underlying reasons for a potential sale, you're also certain to increase the average number of items you can sell to each customer, in a much shorter period of time.

Why is probing, which often causes more grief for salespeople than any other step, so critical? Although we'd all like to believe otherwise, no two customers are exactly the same. It is your job as a salesperson to detect the differences among the customers you serve and to astutely suggest the proper items or alternatives that suit each individual customer.

Suppose two unrelated customers are shopping for new coats. Customer A may be looking for an expensive coat that's appropriate to wear to an upcoming black tie affair, while Customer B may be looking for one that's inexpensive and comfortable for an upcoming hiking trip.

Both customers are looking for the same thing, a coat, but clearly each has a different motive. What will happen if you make the same demonstration to both customers? You'd probably lose one sale and maybe both. On any given day, the inability to probe loses salespeople thousands of dollars in sales and commissions, even though they may have spent substantial time with their customers.

Anyone can ask: "Are you looking for a coat?" and then take the customer to the coat rack and start demonstrating. It takes a professional to find out the personal reasons a customer is looking for a coat and to get the customer to feel like his or her needs are being personally met during a demonstration.

KNOWLEDGE IS POWER

The more you know about your customers, the more you'll be able to help them select merchandise and sell it to them. You'll also be better able to suggest accessories or add-on merchandise that will increase the amount of the sale . . . and your bank account.

Probing is More Than Finding Out Why

Finding out why a customer wants an item is not the only goal of probing. Two additional and equally important goals of probing are:

- To develop an understanding of a customer's wants, needs and desires; and
- To develop the customer's trust in you.

Understanding

Developing empathy and an understanding of your customer's wants, needs and desires or even hopes, dreams and aspirations, requires effort. You need to develop the skill of asking good questions and digging for facts. If a customer is excited about a special event, you need to capitalize on that excitement to help you make or add on to the sale.

If you were shopping for things to take on the most expensive and exciting vacation you've ever been on, wouldn't you want people to listen to you talk about it? Telling people about your vacation plans is sometimes half the fun! So your goal becomes listening, empathizing and getting involved with your customers as much as possible. People really like being listened to, don't they?

Trust

Getting your customers to trust you also takes skill and practice. Establishing trust is a subtle skill. You can't do it by making a presentation too fast or grilling a customer. In probing, indeed, the number of questions you ask is not necessarily relevant to developing trust.

Trust is established through the caring tone of your questions and the empathetic support you give to your customer's answers.

Your customers need to feel that you are genuinely interested in them and in the hopes they have for their purchase. If they don't trust you, you are going to have a difficult time trying to sell them anything. Conversely, if you can develop a trusting relationship between you and your customers, chances are they will value your opinion more highly and buy what you recommend. They may even spend more money than they had originally planned on spending.

Developing Your Probing Skills

To figure out the wants, needs and desires of your customers and to get as many of them as possible to trust you, you need to develop the proper skills. In this chapter, we will discuss three proven methods for understanding your customers' motives to get them to trust you as a salesperson:

- Open-Ended Fact Finding Questions
- Question-Answer-Support (Q.A.S.)
- Logical Sequence

Open-Ended Fact Finding Questions

Imagine you are on the sales floor with two customers who are each looking for a coat. You may now know what differentiates the two customers, but you still don't have all the details. Is Customer A attached to mink? Or will she like different kinds of fur as well? Does she require full-length, or will something shorter be more appropriate?

What about Customer B? What style of coat will she prefer? One with a hood? Or one with lots of pockets for carrying a compass, maps and other hiking necessities? What color does she like and what types of climate will she be wearing it in?

You can find out the answers to these questions and more through the use of "open-ended" questions, which necessitate more than a "yes" or "no" answer from your customer.

The English language has blessed us with six magnificent words and one phrase. They are:

Who   What   Where   Why
When   How   Tell Me

When you start a question with one of these words, or start a sentence with "Tell me," you are more likely to get a complete answer with lots of extra useful information than if you used a closed-ended question such as "Are you," "Could you," "Did you," and so on.

I'm not sure how this happens, but when people get on the selling floor they have a tendency to guess what the customer wants or give the customer choices instead of leaving the questions broad and open. For example:

CLOSED	OPEN
Do you want dressy or casual?	What style do you prefer?
Did you like blue or yellow?	What color do you want?
Are you sure you like that brand?	Why have you chosen that brand?
Do you want one with remote capability?	What features are important to you?
Is it a gift, or for you?	Who are you shopping for?
Is it for a special occasion?	What is the special occasion?
Did you want a collar?	What style of collar do you want?
Do you want it lined?	What type of lining would you prefer?
Do you want it full length?	What length would you prefer?
Are you looking for something special?	What are you looking for?

The point is, that with closed questions, you are less likely to get valuable extra information as to why the customer wants a particular item. Instead you get only *what* they want.

Here is an interesting question for you. What is the most important thing to you in selecting a new car? Before reading any further, take a moment and answer the question. When I ask this question at seminars, the answers I receive are as varied as:

Color • Economy • Resale value • Safety
Speed • Style • Comfort, etc.

All of those answers give us the personal reasons why each person wants the car. Is it possible that all of the people who responded were looking at the same car? The answer is yes. The problem is making a selling point on speed when the customer wants color, or talking about comfort when the customer is only interested in gas mileage. A good prober is curious about why the *customer* wants an item, and why he or she is shopping with you. It is extremely important that you keep your personal reasons for liking or disliking a particular item out of consideration. After all, you are there to serve the customer, not have a forum for your personal opinions.

Just as the doctor asks you questions before prescribing treatment, or a journalist asks questions before an article is written—professional salespeople must have at their disposal the correct questions to open up the customer. Unlike opening, where there are potentially thousands of opening lines, there are a limited number of good probing questions. You will use them over and over. They must be so practiced that you can use them without trying to remember them. Selling on the floor goes too fast for you to try and come up with your next question. It's kind of like seeing a red light and thinking about what to do instead of putting on the brakes.

Listed below are some of the best probing questions I've found. Commit them to memory. I have tried to be as generic as I can; however, you may have to supplement the list with some of your own. The asterisks by certain questions indicate that they are favorites of mine that I believe you should pay particular attention to. In fact, you'll use most of them with practically every single customer.

PROBING QUESTIONS

Who
*Who are you shopping for?
Who will be using it the most?

Who will be helping you with this decision?
Who is the lucky person?
Who do you know that has one already?
Who told you about our store?
Who will be maintaining it?
Who wants it the most?
Who else will be attending?
Who's your favorite manufacturer?
Who else is on your shopping list?

What

*What brings you into the store today?
*What is the special occasion?
*What kind do you have now? (and follow up with)
 What would you like to do this time?
*What features are important to you?
*What have you seen before that you really liked?
 What do you want to accomplish by selecting a
 mattress?
 What color do you prefer (or, colors would blend best)?
 What style do you prefer?
 What do you want it to do for you?
 What size requirements do you have?
 What room will you use it in?
 What kind of look are you trying to achieve?
 What do you do for a living?
 What experience have you had using a camcorder?
 What do you think your husband would like most?

Where

*Where have you seen one before?
 Where will it be used?
 Where will you be traveling?
 Where do you live (or are you from)?
 Where is the special event taking place?

When

*When is the special occasion?
*When have you seen one before that you really liked?

*When did you decide that you had to have one?
*When did you begin shopping?
 When do you want it?
 When was the last time you shopped for lighting?
 When will you use it the most?
 When did you want to start using it?
 When did you have the opportunity to use one last?

How

*How did you hear about us?
*How long have you been shopping for one?
*How would you like your new sofa to look (or, feel)?
 How often do you purchase dive equipment?
 How often do you update your wardrobe?
 How did you decide on this model?
 How often will you use it?
 How often do you like to replace your work clothes?
 How many people will use it?
 How were you going to present it?

Tell Me

Tell me about your husband (wife, kids, etc . . .).
Tell me all about your redecorating (vacation, etc.) plans.
Tell me more about the problems or concerns you have
    had in the past (or, you have now).
Tell me more about. . . .

Why

Why is it that you want wool versus cotton?
Why is it important to have a blue one?
Why are you concerned about the durability?
Why that specific model or brand?

Using "TELL ME"

"Tell me" is a wonderful way to prompt customers to
tell you their life story as it relates to their purchase. Suppose you say, "Tell me about your back yard." Of course
there is a benefit if you are selling casual furniture to find

out how big the patio is so you can make sure the set you are selling will fit. But, more important, it's the extra information you get from the customer at this point that may present you with a greater potential for adding on merchandise or bumping what you have demonstrated to a more elaborate set. For example, you might find out that they are adding on to their deck and a couple of loungers would be really great to go with the basic table and chairs. Or, you might find that a deluxe barbecue or spa is also needed. The possibilities are worth discovering.

Using "WHY?"

I left "why" at the bottom of the list for a reason. Most of the trainers I have come across do not like using "why?" They may believe that it is too personal and may sound too pushy, but nothing could be further from the truth. "Why?" is a clarifier and verifier. If customers come into a shoe store and ask for thin-soled shoes, how can I serve their best interests if I don't ask them why they like thin-soled shoes? What if the customer said, "I'll be standing on my feet all day and I feel I'll be more comfortable with thin-soled shoes." This is great information to have, because what the customer really needs is thick-soled shoes. By asking "why," I clarified the customer's thinking and I'm better able to serve that person. You can soften up the question easily by prefacing it with a phrase like, "You know, I'm curious." Then follow up with your why question. When asked sincerely, the last thing that customers will think is that you're being pushy.

Never Ask the Customer "How Much?"

Have you ever gone into a retail store and fell in love with something and spent more money than you had planned? I know I have. In fact, I've made a specialty of it. If that's the case for you, it is probably the case for your customer as well. Your job is to create a desire in your customers and sell them what they really want. It is not to ask how much the customer wants to spend.

For example, if you ask customers how much they want to spend, they might say $500. On the other hand, what if you simply show them something for $1000? Isn't it possible that they would then say that they won't spend a penny over $750? By golly, that's 50 percent more money than the $500 they would have indicated if you had asked them up front. If you do ask, it limits you like crazy. If they say they want to spend $500 and you show them something for $1000, you risk being perceived as pushy. And if you were to take a scientific approach to this, you'd find that the law of gravity suggests that it's easier to come down than it is to go up. The truth is, the emptier the customer's pocket in the end, the more full yours will be.

Take Care With the Words You Choose

You will remember from the chapter on the precheck that salespeople really have to be painters by using words that express beautifully and clearly. Your words are the difference between sounding like a poet or a truck driver, and subtle choices can make all the difference in the world. For example, you would never use the words "buy" or "need" in your probing questions. Replace the word "buy" with "shop" and "need" with "want." For example, instead of saying, "How long have you been looking to *buy* a sofa?" say, "How long have you been *shopping* for sofas?" And instead of saying, "When do you *need* it?" say, "When do you *want* to start using your new sofa?" Your choice of words can really soften the sound of your questions and even encourage more expressive answers.

Always Be Prepared

I've always thought probing was, in a way, like golf. According to the Professional Golfers Association rules, you're only allowed to carry 14 clubs in your golf bag. Not 15 or 16. A maximum of 14. What percentage of pro golfers carry 14 clubs every single time that they are on the course? How about 100 percent? Of course. Why would pros ever put themselves in the position of not having the best possible club for any particular shot? They absolutely wouldn't. The similarity here is that a professional salesperson would never walk onto the selling floor without having all of the possible probing questions available to use. Probing questions are as important to the salesperson as golf clubs are to the golfer.

Developing Trust

There have been a lot of psychologists and big thinkers who have come up with reasons people are motivated to buy . . . from Maslov to Hertzberg to people with theories on the left brain and the right brain.

I believe that there is merit in any information that will get a better handle on how to communicate with, and sell someone. But because retail moves so fast and because of the resistant nature of customers, I believe we should stick to the simple reasons people buy. There are two: TRUST and VALUE. The customers should trust you and the store, and see value in your merchandise. With trust and value established, a sale is imminent. Value will be discussed at length in the demonstration, but for now let's examine how you can build a trusting relationship with your customer.

People need to be heard and acknowledged. The easiest way to show this premise is to look at a little child tugging at the pants leg of a parent, whimpering or crying or yelling out questions at a mile a minute. The parent, at the same time, is yelling back, "Wait a minute," or "Be quiet," or "Not now." The child just wants to be acknowledged. If the parent were to look the child directly in the eyes and say, "What do you want?", get an answer from the child and deal with it one-on-one, the child would be much more likely to behave, even if it were to just delay the child's immediate request for the moment. Adults are no different.

In the early 80s, I was working for a client in one of his jewelry stores and overheard a sales presentation. What I heard changed the way I have taught selling forever. Here is part of the dialogue:

After schmoozing a little while, the salesperson asked:

Salesperson: What brings you into our store today?

Customer: I was in Hawaii last week and saw the most beautiful necklace I have seen in a long time.

Salesperson: What type of necklace was it?

Customer: It was a. . . .

This dialogue seems simple and logical. After hearing it I realized why I was different, and maybe why I outsold that salesperson and many others. What was wrong with the presentation? A couple of things:

First, why would the customer have mentioned Hawaii if she weren't proud of the fact that she was there last week? The customer was still on a high from the trip and still telling everyone she met that she was there. The salesperson chose not to hear it or didn't think it was important.

Second, there was no support or acknowledgement of the information the customer was volunteering. If the customer didn't want to talk about Hawaii, she would have said, "I saw a necklace last week and I wanted to see if you had one just like it." Let's take a look at how the conversation could have evolved:

Salesperson: What brings you into our store today?

Customer: I was in Hawaii last week and saw the most beautiful necklace I had seen in a long time.

Salesperson: Hawaii? That's a wonderful place. What type of necklace was it?

In this example, you see support for the word "Hawaii" and you begin to see a more personal dialogue build. In opening the sale, I talked about "hanging out." Here is a very vital part of your presentation. Let's take a look at where the salesperson should have gone from there.

Salesperson: Hawaii? Wow! What island were you on?

Customer: Maui.

Salesperson: I'm jealous. How long were you able to stay?

Customer: Two weeks.

Salesperson: You're so lucky. Tell me about Maui. I have always wanted to go there.

She will continue to elaborate on the subject of Maui. She may even dance the hula for you. These few seconds or even minutes are everything to your presentation. In fact, if you were to take the necessary time in probing and hanging out, your entire presentation time would be cut in half. The time wasted in selling is usually in the demo or handling objections when you have no relationship or didn't find out what the customer wanted, and why. Now let me ask you a question. Do you think the second dialogue created a warmer and more attentive relationship than the one that got into business so fast?

Put on your inspiration hat for a moment and play along with this game. Here is the set-up:

Imagine one of your closest friends, someone you really care about. He happens to be single and he is not really dating anyone at the present time.

You are sitting in your living room and there is a knock at the door. You open the door to see your friend standing there. You, of course, invite him in. You then say, "What's happening?"

Your friend replies, "I eloped last night!"

If you really want to have some fun, do this with a friend and simulate the situation. When you are done, it may sound something like this:

You: You eloped last night? Are you crazy?

Friend: Maybe, but I did it.

You: Who was it?

Friend: I met her at a party yesterday afternoon and fell in love.

You: You have got to be kidding. What's her name?

Friend: Janet.

You: Wow! I can't believe this! Where did you get married?

What's the moral of this story? If you notice, all the questions were open-ended and after each answer there is a supportive response. In real life, people who want to know something naturally talk this way. How is it that it all seems to go away once you set foot on the selling floor? Get curious, get caring and watch how your customers will respond!

Q.A.S.

The technique for giving support and hanging out is called Q.A.S. It stands for Questions the customers Answer and your Supportive response. I can't think of a better way to develop and enhance a trusting relationship between you and your customer. Let's take a look at a few examples of probing with and without Q.A.S. and then *you* decide:

Dialogue Without Q.A.S.

Question: So what brings you in today?

Answer: I'm looking for a gift for my son.

Question: Whats the special occasion?

Answer: It's his sixteenth birthday.

Question: When is it?

Answer: Next Tuesday.

Question: What have you got planned for him?

Answer: I think it's more appropriate to ask what he's got planned for himself!

Question: What's he got planned?

Answer: He's going out with some friends to that new dance place that doesn't serve alcohol.

Question: So what have you seen before that he'd really like?

Answer: Well, he's really into video games so I was thinking about getting one of those hand-held games. I've seen them advertised a lot lately.

Question: What kinds of games does he enjoy the most?

Answer: Oh, it's got to be fast action stuff. I like the strategy and logic ones, but he's got no patience.

Dialogue With Q.A.S.

Question: So what brings you in today?

Answer: I'm looking for a gift for my son.

Support:	Well, that's great.
Question:	What's the special occasion?
Answer:	It's his sixteenth birthday.
Support:	Oh, boy! Sixteen years old. That's an important one. Girls, drivers license, job after school.
Question:	When is it?
Answer:	It's next Tuesday.
Support:	Tuesday! Wow, that's coming up fast.
Question:	What have you got planned for him?
Answer:	I think it's more appropriate to ask what he's got planned for himself!
Support:	Uh-oh. No more birthday parties with the family, huh?
Question:	What's he got planned?
Answer:	He's going out with some friends to that new dance place that doesn't serve alcohol.
Support:	I've heard about that place. I think it's great that there's somewhere for kids to go and you don't have to worry about them getting into trouble.
Question:	So what have you seen before that he'd really like?
Answer:	Well, he's really into video games so I was thinking about getting one of those hand-held games. I've seen them advertised a lot lately.
Support:	They're great. People of all ages are really getting into them.
Question:	What kinds of games does he enjoy the most?
Answer:	Oh, it's got to be fast action stuff. I like the strategy and logic ones, but he's got no patience.
Support:	I know what you mean. My reflex time gets longer with every year that I get older.

LOGICAL SEQUENCE

You now have excellent probing questions at your disposal, and you know how valuable supporting the answers to those questions is. Now comes the question, "Which question do I use first, or second?" Like golf, you don't want to putt with a driver or drive with a putter. The subject of order is called "logical sequence." If you look at a funnel, you will see a large opening at the top, which gradually narrows into a small opening at the bottom. Probing is very much like that funnel. You ask broad-based questions at the beginning and move towards very specific questions later.

Questions should be asked in such a way as to first find out *what* customers want and move toward finding out *why* they want it. Then move toward finding out more specifically *which* particular item they want. There are also questions that need to be asked in relation to their knowledge of the merchandise and whether they have shopped for this item at other stores. The first three or four questions asked will set you up with not only those answers, but give you a clear path for the rest of your presentation. In a way, I feel it is a little like boxing. When an opponent moves this way, you move that way. When he swings here, you respond there, and so on. It is never a matter of thinking, it's a matter of reacting. So it is crucial that you role-play as much as you can. No professional ever practices on the public.

After schmoozing, the first probing question is always, "What brings you into our store today?" But where do you go from there?

Question: What brings you into our store today?

Answer: I'm looking for a gift for my husband

Support: That's very thoughtful of you. It's fun looking for gifts.

What's the next question?

As your mental computer searches through your bank of probing questions, there should be only one logical question to ask next:

Question: What is the special occasion?

The reason is that the more important the occasion, the more important the gift. You wouldn't want to make a $100 sale when, because of the occasion, you could have sold $300 worth of merchandise, would you? Besides, even if it isn't for someone else and the customers are shopping for themselves, asking the questions may cause them to tie it to an occasion and still spend more money.

Keep playing:

Question: What is the special occasion?

Answer: It's our 25th wedding anniversary.

Support: Congratulations, what a wonderful accomplishment! It is rare to meet someone who has been married that long.

What is your next question?

The next best question would have to be, "When is your anniversary?" Time is an important factor in selling. Also, the shorter the time the more expensive the gift. People will be willing to spend more if they don't have to shop anymore or you can solve their problem.

Question: When is your anniversary?

Answer: It's this Saturday.

Support: It sure is coming up fast.

"It sure is coming up fast," should be used as a supportive response on any upcoming event of a year or less. "When is the event?" "Two weeks." "Boy, that's coming up fast." "When is the event?" "Six months." "Boy, that's coming up fast." This supportive response cites the penalty for not making a decision today. Anything you can do to hurry up the customer's process of making a decision today is high on my list of things that I like a lot.

Keep playing:

Support: It sure is coming up fast.

What's your next question?

Now you know what the event is, and when. The next

thing you need to know is if the customer has been shopping. So, the next logical question would be:

Question: What have you seen before that you really liked?

Your customer will give you one of two possible answers:

(1) I saw a _____ down the street (or something similar), OR
(2) I haven't looked, (or I just started shopping).

In Number 1, my question is why didn't the customer buy at the other store? And I will ask that question. Yes, I actually will ask, Why didn't you buy it? It's not too aggressive if you ask it with a lot of concern. But I want to know why they didn't go for it in the other store so I make sure it doesn't happen in mine. It's essential. In Number 2, you continue the probing process with a question like, "What do you think your husband would like the best?" This wording is better than asking what she wants to get him. Put the burden on the recipient, who usually wants a better gift than the giver would have thought of.

Even in the carpet business, the portable spa business and other apparent non-occasion businesses, I always follow this sequence. Refer to the chart below as a guide to logical sequence:

LOGICAL SEQUENCE GUIDE CHART

After asking the key transitional question, "What brings you in today?" and while you are still in the opening area of the store, there is a specific list of probing questions that must be asked, in order:

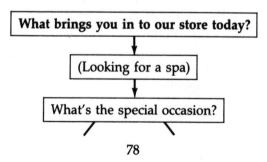

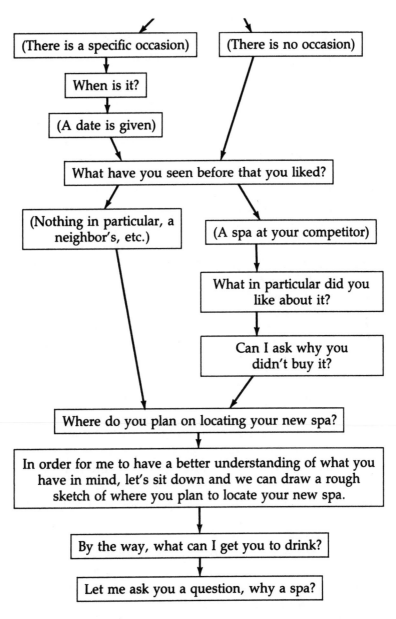

Continue probing using the list of questions found earlier in this chapter, narrowing your search with more specific questions. You want to discover *what* your customers want, then *why* they want it, and then more specifically *which* item they want. Remember to use the Question-Answer-Support format while probing, to really establish customer trust.

SWITCHING—OR SELLING WHAT YOU HAVE FIRST!

A common situation that you may encounter is a customer request for a particular brand you do not carry, a particular item that is out of stock, or an item you don't have in the right size. No retail company can maintain stock levels with every item available, in every size and at any time. The ability to convert a customer from an item you don't have to one that is in stock is one of the most powerful tools you can develop. In fact, there would probably be little, if any, need for salespeople on the floor if all they had to do was show the items requested. If that were the case, you'd be working in a grocery store. Think about it. No shopper in a grocery store ever walked up to some stock person and asked if she could get bigger peas, or carrots that were a little more orange! The only reason salespeople are needed to begin with is because stores generally carry merchandise that not everyone wants!

It is during the probing process that you can best introduce an alternative. Successfully selling an alternative to a customer may get the "right" item into the customer's hands in the first place.

Unfortunately, some customers will not be able to be switched to an alternative no matter what you do. I remember my niece calling me up one day. Knowing that I had a lot of shoe clients, she asked if I could get her a particular style of Reebok athletic shoes that were in short supply because of their popularity. Here are all the facts: she was 16 years old, very popular, and 400 of her closest friends happened to have owned that particular Reebok. Anybody out there want to take a shot at switching her? It would be easier to climb Mt. Everest than to switch her to some other shoe that might satisfy her.

On the other hand, some people might say they want Reeboks because they heard that it was a good brand, yet not be stuck on any particular style. These people are a lot easier to switch. When a customer suggests that he wants a particular brand that you do not carry, ask the question "Which model (style, etc.)?" You can discover whether the customer has been looking and is committed to finding the best possible price, or if he or she is open to other possibilities. For that matter, it is an excellent question to ask even if you do carry the brand requested.

In the event that you do not carry the brand, in order to successfully switch the customer without seeming pushy, there are several steps you should follow:

1) After finding out what customers want, ask "why" they want that particular item. Remember, if they mention a brand or item you don't carry, ask which model and style anyway. Knowing the answer to this question is the key to switching. After the customer answers your question, you must give a supportive response to confirm to the customer that you were listening and that you care. Remember, support builds trust. For example:

Customer: Do you carry Panasony stereo receivers?

Salesperson: That's a great brand. Which model?

Customer: I don't know. I just heard they were good.

Customer: Do you carry Panasony stereo receivers?

Salesperson: That's a great brand. Which model?

Customer: Model 2501.

2) At this point, ask the customer's permission to show an alternative. This will convey a helpful, caring feeling to the customer rather than a pushy, "I want to sell you something else" type feeling. As you are asking permission, you want to explain why you don't have the item requested and why you feel you have an alternative the customer might like. I like to blame it on the buyers.

"You know, our buyers shop the world every year in order to select the best value possible for our customers. Unfortunately, they haven't selected that brand (or model) this year. However, if you like that brand, I know that I have something that you will absolutely love. May I show it to you?"

If the customer agrees to look at the alternative, be sure to point out how it will benefit the customer in the same way, if not better than the requested item. In other words, tie your demonstration points to "why" the customer wanted the requested item.

If your customer declines your offer to show a similar item, you may be in a difficult position. You may potentially run the risk of being pushy by trying to switch unwilling customers. On the other hand, it's difficult not to try and sell them something. The relationship that you've built with the customer at this point will be your best clue as to how to proceed.

The following examples illustrate how to politely and effectively switch the customer to an alternative by using these steps.

Scenario A: A customer walks right up to a salesperson upon entering the store. He immediately asks for a brand the store doesn't carry.

Salesperson: Why have you chosen that particular brand of television?

Customer: My friend recommends them. He is really happy with the picture on his.

Salesperson: Yes, they're a terrific unit. You know, our buyers have the opportunity to choose any brand of televisions available and have not selected that particular brand this year. Based on the fact that you're looking for a good picture, we do have another brand that is very similar and also has something extra that you might like too. May I show it to you?

Scenario B: A customer comes in to purchase a piece of crystal that the store has discontinued and cannot be special ordered. When she doesn't see it, she asks the salesperson where it is in the store.

Salesperson: Sounds like you've looked at it before. What is it that you like about that line of crystal?

Customer:	I just really like the simple, contemporary look.
Salesperson:	Yes, they do have wonderful designs. Unfortunately, our buyers have chosen not to carry that line anymore, but you'll be happy to know they replaced it with an equally contemporary line that you may like as well, if not better. May I show it to you?

Scenario C: A customer finds a shirt that he likes and asks to try it on in his size, but you discover you are out of that style in his size. You have a possible alternative that you would rather sell before resorting to having it transferred from another store or special ordering.

Salesperson:	It is a great shirt, isn't it? Unfortunately, we don't have your size in this style in stock. May I ask you a question?
Customer:	Sure.
Salesperson:	What is it about this shirt that attracted your attention?
Customer:	The color looks like it would match a lot of my outfits.
Salesperson:	It really is a good basic color. I have two other shirts that are very similar in color that you might like even more. May I show them to you?

A Special Idea for Salespeople in Home Decorating or Furnishings

After schmoozing and the transition of, "What brings you into our store today?" the first few probing questions used in logical sequence should be followed. However, the difference is in the way you should probe from this point on. Get your customers seated.

If you can get your customers to sit down at a table with a pad of quarter-inch graph paper and sketch their home, a room, or their back yard, you will not only get answers to your probing questions, but will learn a tremendous amount about what your customers have now and their hopes for the future. We're talking about major purchases here. Taking the time in a comfortable setting to show how much you care will make your customers feel special and more at ease, making it easier for them to talk openly. Remember, while customers are seated, take advantage of every opportunity to "hang out" and build an even stronger rapport.

All in all, I think you will find probing to be one of the most dynamic steps in all of selling. Not only will it save you tons of time, but it gets you the extra information needed to add on and close the sale.

HOT TIPS AND KEY INSIGHTS

- Anyone can find out what a customer wants, but it takes a sales professional to find out why. Knowing the "why" about a purchase can provide you with powerful ammunition to help you close the sale later on.

- In determining why, take the time to understand and express your true interest in the customer's wants, needs, and desires. Do this by asking as few questions as possible, but as many as it takes to obtain the information necessary to select the right item to demonstrate.

- No two customers are exactly the same. It is your job as a salesperson to detect the differences among the customers you serve and to astutely suggest the proper alternatives that suit each individual customer.

- The more you know about your customers, the more you'll be able to help them select merchandise and sell it to them. You'll also be better able to suggest accessories or add-on merchandise that increases the amount of the sale . . . and your commission.

- By attempting to build a trusting relationship between you and every customer that walks through the doors of your store, you will not only maximize your sales potential, you will also develop a large group of devoted customers who will return time and time again to obtain your advice.

- Getting your customers to trust you also takes practice. You can't do it by grilling a customer for answers; indeed, the number of probing questions you ask is not relevant. Trust is established through the tone of your questions and your empathy with the customer.

- To eliminate the guesswork, ask the customer open-ended questions that begin with WHO, WHAT, WHY, WHERE, WHEN or HOW.

- If the setting is conducive, sit down with your customers to prompt conversation. The more comfortable and at ease you are able to make your customers feel, the closer you will be to your customers' inner wants, needs and desires.

- Continue to use some of the open-ended questions that you have been rehearsing, but don't bombard your customers with a flurry of questions. You don't want to confuse them and end up jeopardizing a sale. Learn to ask the proper questions in the proper sequence.

- When you effectively use open-ended questions, you help customers clarify their thinking so that you can better help them to make the purchase that's right for them.

- Keep open-ended questions in your back pocket for use in any given situation. It's not *how many* open-ended questions you ask—but how many *effective* ones you ask.

- It is a mistake to narrow down the customer's choice *before he or she is ready.* Avoid using questions with an "either/or" choice, and don't ask what customers are willing to spend.

- Using the Q.A.S. formula to build trust with customers:

$$\frac{\text{PROBING}}{\text{QUESTION}} + \frac{\text{CUSTOMER}}{\text{ANSWER}} + \frac{\text{SUPPORTIVE}}{\text{RESPONSE}} = \text{TRUST}$$

- While you may not want to become best buddies with all of your customers, it is important to make your customers trust you and feel that you understand what they're saying to you.

- Don't be intimidated by "educated" customers. Strive to establish enough trust so that customers will allow you to assist them in their purchase.

- Probing questions are best asked in a logical order. Otherwise, both you and the customer may be so confused that you never get anywhere.

- You can determine whether customers will be spending a lot or a little, based upon the occasion they're buying for. If the special occasion is taking place in the near future, then you can probably start your customer off at a higher price.

- Abbreviate the probing when your customer knows exactly what he or she wants.

- Since every customer who walks into your store is different, treat each one accordingly during the probing process, and do not stop probing until you have a clear mental picture of what your store has that matches what the customer wants.

- The next time you are out of stock, set up in your mind what you're going to switch the customer to. Blame the store's buying department, but give yourself credit for being wise enough to find something as good or better.

- Probe until you have exhausted your opportunities to either sell merchandise or win a repeat customer. Use your acting skills and make it exciting!

CHAPTER FOUR

THE DEMONSTRATION

**Selling is the most fun when a customer
says, "I'll take it," before you have the
chance to say, "Will you buy it?"**

You have completed the probing process and have shown empathy and caring, learned everything you could about your customers, and built trust. You know what they want and why they want it.

This is the moment of truth: now it really *is* showtime.

The demonstration is the part of the sales process where you get to be creative, be the expert your customers expect you to be and show your stuff. Bring a lot of enthusiasm along, because as the probing ends, the demonstration curtain is opening and you're "on." If you offer a dynamite presentation, developed particularly for the customer's needs, you can win a standing ovation at the cash register.

The Demonstration Follows What You Learned in Probing

Unless your probing has been effective, it is difficult to match the personal wants and needs of the customer, or show why he or she should buy your merchandise. The probing process and the information gathered from it are inextricably linked to your demonstration, and will take on increasing significance as we move through subsequent chapters of this book.

By the time you've completed probing, enthusiasm for your merchandise should have increased so that customers are like kids in a candy store. They can't wait to hear what you have to tell them. You're *not* going to bore them with useless details that will diminish their enthusiasm, but you are going to maintain their excitement by custom-designing the ultimate sales presentation.

Again, customers buy for two reasons: TRUST and VALUE. Trust is established during the probing process. The demonstration is where you introduce value. Establishing value involves much more than justifying price. Research suggests that price may only be a small part of what people look for in the merchandise they buy.

Suppose a customer walks into your shoe store, sees a pair of shoes, turns them over and finds they are priced at $300. You can see the look of astonishment: that's a lot of money for shoes.

During your demonstration, you talk about the shoes' being bench-crafted, which means that one individual is completely responsible for making this pair of shoes. That person selects all the components of the shoes, including the leather, which is exactly matched for both shoes in the pair.

Notice that in describing a process that sounds almost like creating a work of art, the shoes are already taking on value.

You continue: "Since they are bench-crafted, they have the artisan's name on them. When they're finished, the shoes have no nicks, no scratches, and all of the components fit perfectly. Unlike shoes made on an assembly line, these shoes are one of a kind."

You've mentioned all of this in a purely conversational tone, simply offering the customer some fascinating information about where the shoes come from. Yet, the $300 sales tag no longer seems as outrageous as it did when the customer first came in. As value goes up, price seems to come down.

Value can be defined as the total benefits a customer derives from making a purchase. Once a customer understands value, price becomes less important.

In the Mind of the Buyer

Let's face it: **Everything in life is too expensive unless value is attached to it** . . . and value is a personal matter. What is perceived as valuable varies from person to person and even from purchase to purchase. Sometimes value lies in making a purchase to show love. Sometimes it's in finding an investment, having prestige or style or durability, or keeping up with the Joneses.

Some people will pay a great deal for a mechanical or electronic device that is mediocre, just because they like its beauty or the way it's put together—like when I bought a stereo system for my home. It's absolutely beautiful. So beautiful, in fact, that they have one in the Museum of Modern Art in New York City. It has a 40-pound remote control with buttons on its buttons. It's really magnificent—and I know for a fact that I could get a stereo system that sounded twice as good for half the price. But to me, the magnificent beauty of it counts for a lot. Any one or more of these factors may be important to a particular customer with respect to a specific purchase.

What a customer thinks of as value in a purchase may be quite different than what is valuable for another person. We all have buying patterns that may appear schizophrenic but are perfectly logical to us within the framework of our own values. Take Jon Dickens, the vice president of The Friedman Group. A $300 fishing reel? No problem. A $300 pair of shoes that he might wear every single day? I don't think so. "It's just too damn much money."

Customers can buy merchandise anywhere they choose, so if they're talking seriously with you it's because you have communicated empathy and caring during opening and probing. They trust you, and that's important. If customers trust you and can be convinced of an item's value, the chances of making the sale are increased automatically. If customers don't particularly like you but can be persuaded that an item has value, a sale still can be made.

If enough value is not established in the customers' eyes, however, whether or not they trust you, there isn't much chance that they'll buy. We've all bought something before in spite of the salesperson assisting us. But no matter how much we might like a salesperson, if we don't see value in the product, we won't buy it. Stated another way:

Customers don't buy for trust only, but they might buy for value only.

That's why establishing value is essential in making the sale. It's not enough for customers simply to appreciate the value of the product; they also have to be inspired to want it.

Generating the excitement to possess the merchandise is your job, and it cannot be done nearly as well without a showtime demonstration.

Thus, there are two major goals to be accomplished during the demonstration:

- Establishing the value of the merchandise in the customer's mind; and
- Creating a desire within the customer to own the merchandise NOW!

SELLING THE VALUE THAT THE CUSTOMER WANTS

All manufacturers incorporate features to make their merchandise similar to, or different from, another manufacturer's products. The face of a watch may differentiate it from other watches, while all other parts of the watch are similar to many other watches. Clothing might be cut in a style that looks like the work of a particular designer, even though the garment is a "knock-off" of the original. A brand name of furniture has a reputation for withstanding the onslaughts of a young family, and car manufacturers compete with each other to offer the world's longest warranty.

All of the above are features of particular products and they may be what your customer is seeking. Or they may be completely irrelevant.

Features Never Sell—Benefits Do

Customers don't buy features, they buy benefits. Highly successful salespeople carefully choose the points they demonstrate so they can deliver what the customer wants to buy. This is accomplished by matching what you learn in probing to the benefits of the particular merchandise you have available. It can *almost* be stated as an equation:

$$P = A \; D/A$$
Probing = Answers
Demonstrate Those Answers

It is not enough merely to list the various features of a product; what you say about them may be more important than the features themselves. For example, everyone's face has features and people will understand that you are talking about features of the face if you recite what they are: hair, eyes, nose, lips, etc.

Listing features is a "generic approach" to selling. It doesn't require any thought or imagination because you can repeat the same features to anyone. It's almost like telling all of your customers they're buying the best product on the market. Many customers don't believe it, even if it's true, as it's a statement without any personal relevance and it can be said to any customer about any item in the store.

On the other hand, you can create enthusiasm about particular facial features by describing them in a way that paints a picture of them—curly red hair, velvet brown eyes, button nose, luscious lips. Words should be used to creatively depict those aspects of your merchandise that will satisfy the needs your customers have revealed during probing.

91

Words That Persuade

Here is a list of 14 words that are among the most persuasive in the English language. Everyone knows them and they have the advantage of being universally understood. Watch any television commercial tonight and count how many of these words are used. Incorporate them into the language you use in the demonstration—they're the words that cause shoppers to get excited about becoming buyers.

Easy	*Free*
Save	*New*
Love	*Money*
Health	*Results*
You	*Proven*
Your	*Safety*
Discovery	*Guarantee*

These **PROVEN** words are **FREE** and **EASY** for you to use. You'll be communicating with words people **LOVE** to hear and, when **YOU** do, you'll make an important **DISCOVERY**. You'll make more **MONEY**, **SAVE** more time, and improve your **HEALTH** and **SAFETY**. Using these words will **GUARANTEE** you **NEW RESULTS** as a salesperson.

The Value of Product Knowledge Has Its Place

Yes, product knowledge is important and it does have a place. As I said in the precheck, there has always been controversy over what is more important in selling: product knowledge or salesmanship knowledge. I must admit that years ago, I may have been one of those people saying, "If you know how to sell, you really don't need that much product knowledge." I was very wrong. You need them *both*, and if there had to be a choice of which to learn first, it would be product knowledge. However, as a professional, you wouldn't make that choice because you need to know both very well to survive and prosper.

A great demonstration requires your ability to be perceived as an expert. I am sure you will agree that there is nothing more frustrating when you go shopping than to find that you can't get questions answered to your satisfaction.

Product knowledge answers your customer's basic questions. It is also important during your demonstration to offer technical information about your product so that your customers will be aware of your knowledge and see you as the expert. Nevertheless, be careful not to bombard a customer with technical terms or industry jargon, and never be lulled into thinking that product knowledge *per se* can serve as a substitute for presenting the benefits that the customer in front of you needs to see and feel.

Shoppers may feel overwhelmed by complex information or bewildered by language that is unique to your business. Avoid using words or phrases that are familiar to you but could be unfamiliar to customers. You'll only confuse them, and when customers are confused they feel incapable of making an intelligent decision and have a tendency to leave your store.

Occasionally, industry-educated customers may throw a curve by asking a technical question that you can't answer, or requesting details about use or maintenance that are outside your area of expertise. Don't try to wing it. If you don't know, find out so that you can give them the correct information. You'll lose no credibility whatsoever, because there's no disgrace in not knowing, only in not finding out.

If it's necessary, and it's possible, call in the company's "expert." For example, if a customer is concerned about whether a particular woodstove can perform adequately in a large room, you may find it more effective to let the customer speak directly with the service manager or another salesperson who has that knowledge. This will increase customer confidence and add value, because the customer will have conferred with the "general practitioner" and the "specialist" as well.

While technical information may be significant, a little of it can go a long way toward diminishing your demonstration, especially if customers feel that your use of jargon is intended to amaze them about how much you know. Communicate not to show off your knowledge, but to paint a verbal picture of your merchandise within the context of what the customer needs. Use words to *express*, not to *impress*.

Customers want to know, for instance, that opera-length pearls can be worn as a single length, or doubled and used as a choker, "which will give you the versatility you want." They may not care at all about nacre forming in the oyster's shell to make the coating on the pearl. Customers need to hear that XYZ Word Processing Software contains a graphic capability "which will give you an edge with the brochures you are preparing." They may not even understand what a megabyte is.

Here is a list of some words and their jargon to give you an idea:

Shoes	Jewelry	Women's Apparel
Reinforced heel counter	Fluted bezel	Princess-seamed jacket
Combination last	Tiffany mounting	Peplum
Cellular Phones	**Cameras**	**Furniture**
Full spectrum	Low lux	Case goods
Digital compatible	Macro focus	Ozone safe
Computers	**Athletic Shoes**	**China & Glass**
Pixel	Pronation	Bone ash
ROM	EVA	24% PBO
Bicycle	**TV & Stereo**	**Musical Instruments**
Double-butted	Harmonic distortion	Midi capable
Brazon	BNC cable	Over-sampling

It's up to you to make sure the merchandise has personal value for the customer. Remember the equation: get your answers during probing, then make a presentation on those answers. If you have listened carefully to the customers responses in probing, you will have many good points to use during showtime.

Selecting the right feature along with the right advantage and benefit is the ultimate customization of a sales presentation.

When it is done skillfully you will be giving the merchandise a reason for being, therefore giving the customer a reason for buying.

CREATING THE DESIRE FOR OWNERSHIP

It's hard to give the customer a reason for buying, when you don't think much of the merchandise yourself and your negative attitude shines through.

As you get more exposed to the merchandise in your business and acquire more product knowledge, it is difficult not to improve your taste and increase your desire for the "better" things. However, it's deadly in selling if you are not sensitive to the individual taste of each customer.

Many years ago, I was helping a dear friend of mine promote and sell antique porcelain from the People's Republic of China. China had warehouses full of these plates, bowls and vases. Because they were over 100 years old, they qualified as antiques, but weren't particularly that rare. One of the marketing ploys was to take a six-inch plate, put it on a rosewood easel, and attach a beautiful, hand-signed certificate of authenticity. The plate retailed for about $20. I bought a bunch of them to give away as gifts. One friend of mine made it the centerpiece on the mantle above his fireplace. He really thought it was special. Another friend used it as an ashtray.

Another case of value as it relates to taste was when I bought my first car at age 17, a used yellow Ford Falcon station wagon. It was a great car! Was it? At the time, it was to me. Today, I find that my tastes have changed a little and what was good then won't do today. Yet, if I were selling cars and a 17-year-old came in, I might recommend something just like it.

As stressed in Chapter 3, it doesn't matter what you think of the merchandise or what you define as value. The only consideration when you're on the floor is what your customers want and how you can best give it to them.

Inspiring the desire for ownership is an essential part of any demonstration. A woman might appreciate the value of a mink coat, but not necessarily want it. That is . . . until she tries it on. Customers might understand the value of a luxury car, but not want one until they drive it. The same is true of whatever merchandise you sell in your store.

Most of us spend more than we need to spend on consumer goods because we don't always look for practicality.

We *could* buy blue jeans without a brand name embroidered on the rear pocket for a fraction of the price of designer jeans, but which do we buy? We *could* get a four-door sedan instead of a sports car, or $80 shoes instead of $700 boots. Yet, we see something special in these impractical consumer goods and we are inspired to pay for the privilege of owning them.

This is even more the case with high-priced luxury items. An accurate timepiece can be purchased today for as little as $3, so you don't sell a $13,000 watch because it tells time. Customers are motivated to buy the designer watch because they love the way it feels on the wrist, they love the compliments they get, and they enjoy immensely being asked what time it is.

You may think that spending $13,000 for a watch is ludicrous, perhaps as absurd as spending $125 on a pair of air-pump athletic shoes. When 13- or 14-year-old customers come in to buy those shoes, however, it's your job to inspire their parents to want to make the purchase:

> *You know, Mrs. Smith, shoes today are really a lifestyle statement. You and I both know that it's hard to think that any sport shoes in the world are worth $125. But they are worth it in so many different ways. What it means for your son is that he's going to walk into school and not feel isolated from his friends—but feel like he's part of the group.*

> *What is it worth to have your child feel comfortable as part of the social scene? Is it worth the extra $50? I don't know and I certainly can't make the decision for you, but it's an important consideration and you might want to think carefully about it.*

If you are fascinated by what people want, you can inspire them to own the merchandise you are selling. A showtime attitude can make or break the sale.

Being on a Mission

Your customers may be on a "mission" to buy. Are you anything like me? From time to time, I see something that I want so much that it becomes a personal mission to have it. It even becomes difficult to concentrate during the day, knowing I don't have it. Even when I don't have the money, I start to plot, scheme and dream up ways that I can get it.

Here's one of my best. I finally decided, after living in California my entire life, that it was time to get a sports car. And it had to be a convertible. Now I just happen to have a history of hating every car I buy exactly two weeks after I buy it and kicking myself in the pants for not getting the one I really wanted. I decided this would not happen again. After much pain and anguish, I decided on the car that was so great that it would be the last car I would buy for the rest of my life. And even though it was more money than I should spend, could spend or wanted to spend, it would be okay, just this once.

I took along Brad Huisken, national sales manager of The Friedman Group, for moral support. And let's face it, I've trained him over the years to tell me I make good decisions. He was not brought along to discourage me. We walked onto the showroom floor and there it was: a brand-new, shiny, gleaming, hot, leather-smelling, Porsche Cabriolet. And of course, the top was down. I'm not sure, but I think the car said, "Hi, Harry!" The salesperson was expecting me because I had called earlier. And what happened next was most amazing. The salesperson pulled out the keys and said, "Here, take it for a drive." I said, "No way." He said, "Why?" I said, "Because then I'd buy it." He said, "Isn't that why you came here?" I looked at Brad, Brad looked at me—my head bowed, my tail between my legs—and I said, "Yup."

What was so wonderful about this presentation, or lack of presentation rather, was that he chose not to tell me that it was fast. I knew that. Or that it would be fun having a convertible on a hot day. I knew that. Or that it took corners very well. I knew that. Or it had full-leather seats. I could smell that. There was nothing that he could tell me about the car that I didn't know after countless hours of drooling over pictures and specifications of it in magazines. I was on a mission. And lucky for him, he didn't stop me from achieving my goal.

I'm sure you can relate to this story about being on a mission. Just remember that a lot of the time your customers are on missions, too. Try not to stop them from reaching their goals.

COVERING ALL THE BASES

The demonstration technique itself, which is described later in this chapter, enables you to express features and benefits to the customer effectively and entails a series of actions that follow one right after the other. Several additional elements, however, weave through the entire demonstration, and need to be fully understood to ensure success. Because they are so important to the process, and because they are subtle, use of these elements can make or break your presentation. Commit them to memory; they will help you maneuver artfully through an imaginative, inventive and original presentation:

- Save Important Features for Later
- Get the Customer Involved
- Create a Little Mystery

Saving Important Features for Later

You are talking with a customer. Your probing has been completed and you understand clearly what will give that shopper value. There is merchandise in your store with benefits that will address all of your customer's needs. Moving confidently into the demonstration, you match as many of your customer's desires as you can to what the product offers. Your presentation is going well, so you list several other aspects of the merchandise while you're at it.

Suddenly, the customer offers an objection to the purchase and you find you have nothing left to say. You have run out of gas. If you have already told the customer everything you know about the merchandise, where do you go from here?

A skillful demonstration does not involve reciting all of the things you can think of about a product and then hoping. A good demo means delivering a portion of what the customer wants, based on what you've discovered in probing and holding some back. Don't leave yourself without anything to say; choose your demonstration points and *then hold the best ones back*. If your best material isn't required to make the sale you won't have to go to the trouble of using it. If more information is needed to overcome an objection, you will have it at your disposal. Sometimes, offering customers one more huge benefit (I call them cannons) will push them over the edge and make the sale.

It's not unlike negotiation. You go with your very best offer right out of the gate and then have nowhere to go when they want to negotiate for a better price. The process is over.

The next time you show a product or talk about a service, think of the most impressive thing about it and see how long you can go without talking about it. It is a great exercise for learning this type of control.

Getting the Customer Involved

The benefits of the product you are showing are easier to appreciate if people are allowed to experience them for themselves. To maintain your involvement with the shopper, and to get the shopper involved with the merchandise, encourage hands-on participation as you demonstrate the product. Customers who become involved in the demonstration have an increased desire to own the merchandise.

Let customers be captivated by the item. Invite them to push the buttons, turn the knobs, take it for a ride, touch it, feel its quality, see how it looks on them. As you demonstrate, explain how to use the product, as if you were teaching someone how to use it after purchasing it.

Urging customer involvement in the demonstration is particularly effective when the sales counter is eliminated as a tangible and psychological barrier. If your situation permits, walk around to the customer's side and stand next to him or her while showing the product. Your physical position will make it easier to help customers try things on or learn a product's functions. Moreover, customers may perceive your behavior positively, as a willingness to give service.

I liken it to going to an event where there's dancing. You have fun at some of them and some are a drag. I contend that there is a direct relationship between the amount of dancing you did at the event and how much you liked it. If you danced a lot, you loved it. If you didn't dance at all, you hated it. If your customers get to push the buttons and program the VCR themselves, they love the VCR. If you operate it for them and they're not involved at all, they may not like it nearly as well.

When shoppers participate in the demonstration, they develop an emotional commitment to having the merchandise. This commitment, in turn, boosts the customer's trust in you, expands the value of the merchandise to the customer, and increases the customer's desire for ownership.

Salespeople sometimes forget how exciting it is for customers to come in and shop in their stores. For those of us who work around the same merchandise every day, the glow and excitement sometimes wear off with the passage of time, and even expensive pieces may no longer seem special. These feelings of indifference have led some salespeople to handle their merchandise nonchalantly and give lazy demonstrations.

Casual treatment of the products you sell will not move customers to buy them. It may be old hat to us, but customers are seeing the merchandise for the first time. To them it's virgin territory, and how you handle the product will give a positive impression or a negative one. The more care we take in presenting the merchandise, the more value we create in customers' minds.

On the other hand, there are some salespeople that are so intimidated by the merchandise that it never gets touched or brought out of the case. I remember doing a seminar for a major southern California department store's china, crystal and gift department. One of the props for me to use in making my points during the seminar was a huge two-foot porcelain fish. It was very fragile, incredibly unattractive and sold for $600. During the seminar, I picked it up, tucked it under one of my arms and kept it there as if it were a pet. I was really just trying to be funny, but as a result of my handling this fish and showing people that it was touchable, the salespeople in attendance gained the confidence to touch it as well. The result is that they sold more of these fish in the three weeks following the seminar than they had in their two-year history of carrying it.

Tips, Tricks and Special Demo Techniques

It never hurts to tease customers a little by making them wait to see the merchandise while you talk glowingly about it. For example, you could say, "I've got the ring for you," take the ring out of the showcase and hold it in your hand wrapped reverently in a polishing cloth. While you are "polishing" it underneath the cloth, you say:

You are going to love this ring. One of the nice things about it is that the stone is set in four prongs and because of that, the light shines down into it and up through it, which ads a lot of brilliance to the stone. It gives the illusion that it's almost twice as big as it really is. That would be nice, wouldn't it?

Before your customer has even seen the product, value has been added. And as value goes up, the customer's perception of the price goes down. It would be hard to hide a tractor under a polishing cloth, but even large items can be kept out of the customer's sight while you create some mystery about them. If the product you're showing is on the other side of the store, slowly saunter over to it while talking about it. Don't be in a hurry and pace what you're saying to conclude just as you reach the item. Then offer it with a wave of the arm and invite the customer to become involved with it.

If it's possible, isolate the item you're discussing from other items in the immediate area. For example, when the ring is placed on the display pad, the pad not only highlights the piece you're showing, but blocks the customer's view of the other items in the showcase. If the product is large, perhaps it can be moved to an isolated part of the store before you bring the customer to it.

Showing Million Dollar Items

Manipulate the merchandise carelessly and you will convey indifference to the customer. Handle it respectfully and you will increase its value. If you believe every item you have in your store is worth a million dollars, would you treat it differently? Wouldn't that ring be handed to the customer with two hands? Wouldn't the clothing be pulled off the hanger as if it were worth something?

Selling is very physical and emotional. Every industry has special ways to demonstrate its product to increase desire—from working the dressing room and the mirror in clothing, to the customer's selecting music from a salesperson's demo kit in stereos, to a customer's test-riding a bicycle, to the way you get a customer to lie down on a waterbed. It's well worth the investment of time to create a demonstration that really lets customers know how much you love the merchandise and how exciting it will be for them to own.

THE ULTIMATE DEMONSTRATION TOOL

When I was 18 years old, I took my first formal sales-training class. During the class, they taught a method for making a demonstration using features and benefits. The instructor stated that even though features differentiate products and make them special, it is the benefit that customers are looking for. It was a marvelous technique and changed the way I sold, until I read that other trainers were using an advantage as a bridge between the feature and the benefit to describe why that particular feature would benefit the customer.

After looking at that system and studying it for quite a while, I realized that even though it was difficult to learn how to put a FEATURE-ADVANTAGE-BENEFIT statement together, it was well worth the time and effort since it established me as an expert and enabled me to communicate that clearly to the customer.

In addition to the FEATURE-ADVANTAGE-BENEFIT statement, I have added a GRABBER, making it an FABG. The grabber is merely a restatement of the benefit as a question to gain agreement from customers that it will indeed benefit them. I spend an extraordinary amount of time in this chapter talking about FEATURES, ADVANTAGES and BENEFITS because I'm sold on their impact.

During probing, you discovered that the customer has several requirements that will be satisfied by certain features of your merchandise. Tailoring the merchandise's features, advantages and benefits to the needs or desires of your customers is the name of the game. Be careful to avoid merely reciting a list of what the product *has* and don't forget to hold back some material for use later.

The Transition

The transition into the demonstration should set the customer up for anticipation and excitement. Such as:

I've got something you're going to love. It's right over here.

We just received the perfect gift for your wife. Come, let's take a look.

Are you ready? You're going to think this is just perfect.

Not only are these effective transitional lines, they have a tendency to remind you that it's showtime.

The transition to the product should be in generic terms, saving your descriptions for the feature-advantage-benefit-grabber technique you will use next.

"I'd like to show you this ring, coat, hat, sofa, dress, bicycle." If you say "Diamond ring, fur coat, cowboy hat, silk dress, all-terrain bicycle," in the introduction, you will be giving a feature away without explanation. Features shouldn't be given without a corresponding advantage and benefit, as it may cause confusion.

Beginning Your Demonstration

I believe very strongly in starting your demonstration with the phrase, "One of the nice things about these shoes is . . ." or "One of the great things about this phone is . . ." or "One of the terrific things about this computer is . . ." It implies that there are many nice things about those shoes. It is a simple phrase and really sets up the demonstration to be special. And since you won't just be reading off a list of features, it gives the customer comfort to know there are other great things about the item.

Features, Advantages and Benefits DEFINED

To learn the system of features, advantages and benefits, I will use a pair of shoes, since every human being on earth has bought at least one pair of shoes so I know you're familiar with them.

Feature: Features may be a conspicuous part or characteristic of the item or service: what it is made of, where it is made, its color, size, the materials used and so on. Every item in the world is composed of various features the manufacturer selected to be similar to or different from the competition's.

Picture a shoe. You can look at it as a "group of features." Let's take a look at some of them: black, leather, loafer, leather lining, heel cap, made in the U.S.A., hand-stitched, etc. There are many others, but this will be a good start. However, as a painter, it's your job to create a picture that creates desire by using words that produce excitement. Wouldn't it sound much better like this?

Feature
jet black
calfskin leather
traditional loafer
full leather lining
rubber heel cap
proudly made in U.S.A.
carefully hand-stitched

Advantage: The advantage is tied directly to the feature. It could be said it is the gain you will get by having that feature versus *not* having that feature. Some people like to say the feature and then "which means," which will also get you the advantage.

Feature	*(which means)*	Advantage of the Feature
jet black		neutral color
calfskin leather		molds to shape of foot
traditional loafer		will stay in style
full leather lining		finished feel
rubber heel cap		prevents slipping
proudly made in the U.S.A.		quality craftsmanship
carefully hand-stitched		artisan's touch

Special note: Any feature can have several different advantages. For example, although calfskin leather will mold to the shape of your foot, it is also a porous material that allows the shoe to breathe. How do you determine which advantage to use? I'll accept a one-word answer— probing.

Benefit: The benefit is tied to the advantage, not the feature. It could be said that it is the benefit of the advantage, since advantages vary from customer to customer. A benefit by definition is "What will the advantage do for the customer?" Why will it be good to have? What will it do? Again, using the words "which means" in between the advantage and the benefit helps your construction. When you are practiced and confident, you will want to drop "which means" for a smoother flowing FAB.

Just as in selecting the most appropriate features (and advantages) for your customers, there may be several different benefits for each advantage. Again, they should be selected based on probing:

Feature (which means)	Advantage (which means)	Benefit
jet black	neutral color	goes with everything
calfskin leather	molds to your foot	custom-made feel
traditional loafer	will stay in style	wear for years to come
full leather lining	finished feel	comfortable instantly
rubber heel cap	prevents slipping	safety
proudly made in U.S.A.	quality	confidence
carefully hand-stitched	artisan's touch	you'll feel special

Grabbers: The finishing touch

When you go through the exercise of putting together a custom-created FAB for a particular customer, and ending it with a wonderful benefit, doesn't it make sense to see if indeed they think it will benefit them? Grabbers appear at the end of an FAB for just that purpose. It merely involves restating the benefits as a question, to get a positive response.

Many salespeople over the years have felt that the grabber was a little awkward sounding. I agree it is unusual. However, your customers appreciate it and it keeps them involved. And by the way, it works.

When you first get started, you may want to repeat the benefit in full as a grabber. Later, with more experience you can change it to really customize your presentation to the customer.

Item: Hula-hoop

Feature: Perfectly round

Advantage: Easy to spin

Benefit: You'll have a lot of fun

Grabber: You do like to have fun, don't you?

Grabber: Sounds like fun, doesn't it?

Grabber: Sounds great, doesn't it?

Putting it All Together

Understanding the parts of an FABG and how to tailor it to the needs and wants of your specific customer is a tremendous tool. But the real fun comes when you put it all together.

Let's see what a well-constructed FABG would sound like in a real-life situation. This time, we'll demonstrate a piece of fine jewelry:

Salesperson: Based on what you told me, I think this ring would be an excellent choice. One of the nice things about this ring is that the center stone is completely surrounded by diamonds. That makes for a stunning accent to the blue of the sapphire and gives it a look of elegance. You do want the look of elegance, don't you?

Customer: Oh, yes.

Salesperson: Here, let's slip this on. Hey, it's almost a perfect fit. You may not even have to get this sized! Another nice thing about this ring is that the sapphire is from Sri Lanka, where some of the world's finest sapphires come from. It's nice to know you've got the best the world has to offer, especially since you're making an important decision concerning a quality piece of jewelry, don't you agree?

Notice that the salesperson begins by referring to the item simply as "this ring," stating only that it would be an excellent choice. What comes next is the description of the first feature the salesperson offers for the customer's consideration, using expressive words that paint a picture.

There is no discussion of how many diamonds there are in the ring, or technical information about the carats of the gemstones. Instead, the salesperson talks about the benefits of the sapphire being "completely surrounded by diamonds." Why is this a benefit? Because it offers the advantage of having the diamonds serve as a "stunning accent" to the sapphire's color.

The salesperson also has offered to help the customer slip the ring on her finger, and perhaps has even come around to the customer's side of the counter as a preferable place from which to do the demonstration. When the ring is placed on the customer's hand, the salesperson speaks of it as if it's already purchased: "You may not even have to get this sized!"

By this simple act, four important aspects of the sales process have taken place. The salesperson has:

1. Invited the customer to participate with the merchandise by encouraging her to touch the item and try it on;
2. Maintained personal involvement with the customer by standing next to her while slipping the ring on her finger;
3. Referred to the merchandise as if the customer were already committed to it; and
4. Simultaneously, started another FABG by matching a feature of the ring to a need of the customer.

A single feature of an item may have many different benefits and advantages. For example:

Item: House

Feature: Four bedrooms

Advantage #1:   One bedroom could be used as a study.

Benefit #1:   Quiet place to work on weekends.

Grabber #1:   That would be convenient, wouldn't it?

Advantage #2:   All three children get their own room.

Benefit #2:   Privacy for every family member.

Grabber #2:   That would please everybody in your family, wouldn't it?

No matter how many benefits or advantages a feature has, keep your FABG simple. Each FABG needs to contain one Feature, one Advantage, one Benefit and one Grabber. At a maximum, you want to use only the ones that focus on the specific needs of the customer that were covered during your probing. At a minimum, you want to sell the merchandise using the least amount of information possible.

Checking FABGs

Once you have constructed an FABG, there is a check you can use to make sure it is correct. Using the hula-hoop example, start with the feature and work down to the benefit, inserting the phrase "which means" in between each:

"The hula hoop is perfectly round, *which means* it's easier to spin, *which means* you'll have more fun using it."

> **Item:**   Hula hoop
>
> **Feature:**   Perfectly round (which means)
>
> **Advantage:** Easier to spin (which means)
>
> **Benefit:**   You'll have fun

Next, start with the benefit and work up to the feature, asking "why" after each.

"You'll have fun. *Why?* Because it's easier to spin. *Why?* Because it's perfectly round." Since the logic works in both directions, the FABG constructed to demonstrate the hula-hoop is sound.

You Can FABG Anything

One of the nice things about using an FABG approach to demonstrating is that it's a good way to organize your thoughts and enthusiasm about the product and convey them to the customer. When customers can feel the enthusiasm in your presentation, it prompts them to want to buy. And you do want customers to buy, don't you?

The preceding paragraph was brought to you by FABG. It's actually an FABG on FABGs, which proves the point that you can do an FABG on anything. Here are some other examples:

I'd like to show you this suit. Feel that fabric? One of the nice things about this suit is that it's stitched, not fused, which means that all the pieces are actually sewn together, rather than glued down. So, as you wear it and get it cleaned, it will keep its shape. Five years from now it's going to look as good as the day you bought it. That's important, when you invest in fine men's clothing, isn't it?

You know, I picked out this baseball glove for you. Here, take a closer look. One of the nice things about this glove is that it has calfskin on the inside and cowhide on the outside, so it doesn't sting your palm as much and you'll enjoy playing a lot more. You'd rather be thinking about how to catch the ball instead of how much it might hurt when you catch it, wouldn't you?

Here's a sofa I know you'll love. Go ahead and have a seat. One of the great things about this sofa is the soft stuffing used in the back cushions. When you sit back, you really sink right into the cushion, making for great comfort. I bet you can just picture yourself falling asleep here many a night, can't you?

Now, it's your turn. It's important for the spontaneity and individualization of the demonstration, that you learn the system for putting FABGs together, rather than committing a few of them to memory. If you memorize several

109

FABGs to use repeatedly, you won't be finding the value for each customer and you won't be matching the customer's need with the product's features.

Have some fun while learning, by playing the FABG game with co-workers. We do in our company. It's not unusual to hear someone say, while ordering lunch, "One of the nice things about the hamburgers here is the sesame seed bun, which adds a burst of flavor to every bite, making your lunch that much more enjoyable. You guys want to have a great lunch, don't you?" And it wouldn't take more than a couple of seconds for someone else to say, "And another great thing about eating here is the extra large napkins, which provide extra clean-up potential, keeping you looking great while you're eating that burger. Looking good while eating is important, isn't it?" Pick an item at random and rotate, each giving FABGs until one of you wins.

Giving Possession in the Demo

The most recent change to our program resulted from a realization of the value in describing the merchandise as if the customer already owned it. It's sort of a postulate demo. Let's take a look at a simple FABG, one merely describing an item and another giving possession.

Describing: "One of the nice things about this piano is the high-gloss finish, which is a snap to dust off and keep clean, making it a gorgeous centerpiece. That would be nice, wouldn't it?"

Giving possession: "You know, Mrs. Smith, having this particular piano, you're really going to appreciate the fact that its high-gloss finish will be a snap to dust off and keep clean, making it the gorgeous centerpiece you expected it to be in your home. And you know how proud you'll be when everyone compliments you on how great it looks, don't you?"

It's truly an act of persuasiveness. It shows our confidence and desire to make the deal.

AVOIDING THE COMPARISON TRAP

Have you ever been put into the position of comparing two items to a customer and having it result in no sale at all? Or how about you as a customer having a salesperson tell you that the item you're looking at is not good enough, and the one over here is better? Any way you look at it, comparing items in your store is a trap that can cost you sales and commissions. There are a couple of things to consider before you handle a customer's request for comparison: One, any time you put down any item in the store, you're really saying that the store carries things that are not good. Two, comparing items is also *subjective*. In other words, it's your *opinion* that it's better, or more, or greater. A simple example could be two-month, sixteen-event programming on a VCR. Is it better than the one-week, three-event VCR when you consider the customer wants a VCR for playing rented video tapes only? Another potential danger is beating up a $500 item on the way to selling a $1000 item, just to find out that the customer only has $500 to spend. The rule in these cases is *never compare*.

Sell Each Item On Its Own Merit

A better solution is to focus on the value inherent in each item. This can be done by saying, "Item A is good because. . . ," and "Item B is good because . . ." As you explain, offer Feature-Advantage-Benefit-Grabbers to describe what you mean. For example, one fireplace might be extremely efficient, while another one might have a unique design.

By pointing out these differences, but avoiding the trap of saying that one is better, you can guide customers into making a decision based on the features and benefits that will best suit their needs. Then, if customers decide that their budgets can only handle the lower-priced merchandise, there is no "lower quality" comparison to overcome.

Sometimes customers ask why there is a difference in price between two similar items. In this case, simply explain that the features found in the more expensive item may cost more to produce and therefore the price is higher for the finished product. Explain that the quality of materials, workmanship, attention to detail, even brand names are all characteristics that have an impact on price.

Consider two sweaters that appear similar on the surface, but one costs $100 more than the other. The higher-priced sweater might be hand-knitted, as opposed to the other, which is machine-made. That doesn't mean the less expensive sweater is no good; it simply has different qualities. Or, think about the difference in price between a limousine and a family station wagon. If the station wagon was "no good" based on the price difference, everyone would be driving a limousine or riding the bus. Wouldn't you rather sell a station wagon than no car at all?

Here is a scenario where the salesperson is asked to make a comparison between two similar pieces:

Customer: Which wall unit is better?

Salesperson: Well, they both have outstanding features. One of the nice things about this rosewood piece is its uniqueness. You're not going to find many like this so yours would stand out and be noticed. I think you're the kind of person who likes getting compliments, aren't you?

Customer: Yes, I like something that's different.

Salesperson: One of the nice things about this other wall unit is the special hinges in its doors, which are made to withstand a lot of wear and tear. That's important when you're thinking of buying a fine piece of furniture, isn't it?

Customer: Yes, but why is this one so much more expensive?

Salesperson: Well, sometimes the features on a piece cost more to produce and that can have an impact on the price. In this case, I think it's the stained glass in the doors and the hand-carving along the top that's causing the major difference.

Customer: The rosewood piece is a handsome unit, isn't it?

Notice how the salesperson resists being caught up in the customer's desire for comparison. Offered the viewpoint that similar products have different qualities, but are not "better" or "worse," many customers will choose features and benefits over their concerns about price.

So, don't kill the customer's enthusiasm for any of your merchandise by making comparisons. Every product has special features that set it apart; find out the unique attributes of *your* merchandise, and build on them.

Asking Your Opinion

In a lot of selling situations, it will get down to the point where the customer asks you for your opinion. Let's say you've made clear the features and benefits of each and your customers have not indicated which one they want. I highly recommend that you then help them decide on the one *you* feel will most satisfy them, regardless of its price. Let's face it, if you recommend the higher-priced one and they say no, you're no further ahead. If you can make the sale without voicing your opinion, you would be much better served.

Still, sometimes there are situations in clothing, jewelry, shoes, sporting goods and the like, where your opinions can be used to establish credibility by telling your customers how much you don't like an item. For example, suggest that a woman try on a particular blouse because you think it might look great on her, just so you can end up saying, "That's absolutely the wrong color for you. Take it off immediately." Now she's more likely to have confidence in you when you do tell her she looks great. It's the old "have them try on something ugly, so you can tell them it's ugly, so they'll trust you" technique.

Also, it is a wise salesperson who avoids making negative comparisons with the competition. Bad-mouthing others is unnecessary; it lowers you and it makes customers feel uncomfortable.

THE EXPERT KILLS THE DEAL

Now and then customers will bring along a friend or relative who they consider to be more of an expert on

113

the items they're shopping for. This can be a frustrating experience for you, and if you're not careful it can crush the effectiveness of your demonstration.

To handle this situation, first let's acknowledge the reason a customer brings an "expert" along:

- Customers who do not know much about the kind of merchandise you sell may worry about being taken advantage of, and need the expert friend to prevent them from making the wrong choice.

- Sometimes customers like being complimented on their purchases; the compliment serves as a confirmation that they made a wise decision.

- Expert friends may offer to come because they genuinely want to help.

Whoever the experts are, they have, in a way, been "hired" to give their "valuable" opinion. They took the time to get in the car, drive to your store and walk in. And if you don't keep them involved throughout the presentation, they will give an opinion at the very end and it generally will be "No!" If the experts just go along without having any input, they will think they have wasted their time. And nobody wants to waste time.

Watch out, though! Experts who are prone to jealousy may want to ensure that the customer doesn't end up with better merchandise than their own, or may simply want to put you down.

Whatever the case may be, your objective is to sell the merchandise to the customers while simultaneously getting agreement from the expert friends. The simplest way to achieve this goal is by pointing out the Feature, Advantage and Benefit to the customer, and directing the Grabber, which is designed to gain agreement, to the expert.

Suppose the customer and the expert friend have come in to purchase a "pro quality" bicycle. The expert friend has convinced the customer that a pro bike is not the way to go because the customer doesn't do enough cycling to spend that kind of money. You, of course, want the bigger sale.

Say to Customer:	One of the nice things about this particular bike is that it's on the low end of the pro price scale, so you can have the advantages of a pro bike for less money. At the same time, you'll have a bicycle that will grow with your needs.
Say to "Expert":	And wouldn't you agree that it makes sense to get the best quality you can afford now, rather than regret you passed it up a few months from now?

In situations where experts do have expertise or technical knowledge, the simplest way to shut them down is by using an FABG that is so technical that they can't argue with it because it's beyond them. They will agree because they don't want to show their friend that they're not as expert as they contended.

Say to Customer:	One of the nice things about this reel is the new heat resistant drag washers that won't bind or burn up when that big one's peeling line off your reel.
Say to "Expert":	And it's about time that they came up with that new technology, wouldn't you agree?

While you are demonstrating the merchandise, remain completely neutral. Allow the customers and their "experts" to be right. Sometimes the customers decide to go with their friend's advice. If so, begin writing up the sale. This gets the buying decision and the commitment for the purchase on paper.

Before completing the transaction, however, if you still want to bump, point out one more thing. Then, and only then, diplomatically explain the possible problem with the customer's choice. By getting a commitment on paper before approaching the customer, you have let the customer and the expert "win." Subconsciously, the customer is now off the hook and free to change the decision in accordance with your advice.

Example: "You've selected a very good bike, and you've obviously given it a great deal of consideration. There may be only one other factor to think about before you make your final choice. Bike 'B' has a wider range on its cluster, which will make it easier to peddle on inclines and make your ride more enjoyable. And since you live in an area with a lot of hills, you do want your biking experience to be more enjoyable, don't you?"

When customers using "expert" advice still cannot be swayed, you have done all you can to ensure that they make a purchase they won't regret. If you cannot convince them, sell them the merchandise they've chosen. You gave it your best shot. Now give them what they want.

When the Expert Is *In Absentia*—Not There

Sometimes customers don't bring their expert friends with them, only the "sound advice" the expert friends provided. When the "sound advice" isn't sound, you may find yourself in a difficult position. You don't want the customers to buy the wrong merchandise, but you don't know how to tell them that without discrediting their "expert" and having them leave the store without a purchase.

When this happens, make every effort to find out who their consultant is. There's a big difference between the advice they take from a brother and something they heard while in line at the supermarket. Once you know who the expert is, you'll have a better idea whether there is any hope of changing the customer's mind.

Let's say I don't know anything about computers. I ask my brother what I should purchase for my home. He tells me that I should buy an IMB. I go to my local computer store and the salesperson asks me what I need. I, of course, say that I am looking for a computer, an IMB computer. He asks what I am going to do with it; I reply it's for work at home. He then tells me that he has a better, faster and cheaper unit that will be better than an IMB. I now have a choice of whom to believe: my brother, whom I trust, or a salesperson at a retail store who I don't know. You guessed

116

it: I choose my brother. Even if the salesperson were correct, there was no way I was going to listen to him.

To handle this better, first find out where the customer's information is coming from. Then get permission to make the switch:

Salesperson: What brings you in?

Customer: I'm looking for a computer.

Salesperson: What have you seen that you like?

Customer: I just started shopping, but I think an IMB.

Salesperson: That's a great brand. Why an IMB?

Customer: My brother knows about computers, and he recommended the brand.

Salesperson: How does your brother use his computer?

Customer: He uses his at work.

Salesperson: They are very popular for the work environment.

At this point, ask why he wants a computer in detail. After getting his reasons for wanting a computer, try this:

Salesperson: As you know, computer technology changes rapidly. Your brother may not know that some of the less known and smaller companies produce products that really give IMB a run for their money in terms of value. Which makes sense, because they are not as big and they really have to do something special to get your business. I'm sure if your brother knew of these computers he would want to have one for his home as well. May I show them to you?

If the customer says yes, his brother is out of the picture and the customer is showing that he trusts you. If at this point the customer says, "No, I want an IMB," thank him and tell him about support and future business, because this mountain may be too tall to climb.

Occasionally, the customer's "expert" turns out to be a salesperson at your competitor's store, who has given the customer incorrect information. Even if the customer was given misinformation by an unethical competitor, don't knock down the other guy's company or product.

As you can see, opening, probing and now the demonstration are linked to make a supportive, caring and efficient presentation. All along the way, you'll have to insert your personality, style and enthusiasm to create a presentation that will result in the customer's saying, "I'll take it."

HOT TIPS AND KEY INSIGHTS

- The demonstration is the moment of truth—the part of the sales process when you get to be creative and do your stuff. Its success depends in large measure on the thoroughness with which the probe was accomplished.

- Customers buy for two reasons: trust and value. Trust needs to have been established in the probe; value is established in the demonstration.

- Value can be defined as *the total benefit a customer derives from making a purchase.* This is different from the price of the item. It includes anything the customer defines as value in general, or as value in the particular purchase.

- The two major goals to be accomplished during the demonstration are establishing the value of the merchandise in the customer's mind and creating a desire within the customer to own the merchandise.

- Customers don't buy features, they buy benefits. A feature is something the merchandise *has*; a benefit is something the feature *does* for the customer.

- To discover what benefits the customer, match what you learn in the probe to the benefits of the merchandise available. Probing tells you what you need to highlight in the demonstration.

- The demonstration hinges on several elements that weave through the entire presentation, including holding back most of your points to counter later objections, getting customers to participate in the demonstration and creating a mystery about the product to increase its allure.

- The heat of the demonstration is the FABG, the Feature-Advantage-Benefit-Grabber method of presenting the merchandise. This means, for each FABG, choose one **Feature** of the item, state the **Advantage** of having the feature rather than not having it, define a **Benefit** that states what the advantage will do for the customer, and offer a **Grabber** by restating the benefit as a question to gain the customer's agreement.

- FABGs may be constructed for any item. It's a good way to organize your thoughts for the customer and maintain enthusiasm.

- Avoid being trapped into comparing merchandise: every item is best sold on its own merit. Differences in price can be explained by variations in materials and workmanship.

- If customers bring in their own "experts" to judge your merchandise, handle them politely but firmly. Sell the item to the customer while getting agreement from the "expert."

- Avoid criticizing rival companies or manufacturers. Discrediting competing merchandise always backfires because your negative tone creates a negative atmosphere for customers.

- Your goal with every shopper is to turn him or her into a buyer, using the only expert advice that counts—yours.

CHAPTER FIVE

THE TRIAL CLOSE
(Otherwise known as the Assumptive Add-on Close)

**Making a presentation without
a close is like writing a novel
without a final chapter.**

When I first developed the seven-step selling process, one of the steps I used was borrowed from the world of industrial selling, called "the trial close." The purpose of this step, used by business-to-business salespeople, is to gain minor positive decisions or to test the waters with customers, to see if they are ready to buy. It made some sense then, but it doesn't now, particularly for retail selling.

What you did in this step was to ask your prospects to make a minor decision. For example, "Do you want to pick up the products at the factory, or have them shipped?" or "Do you want to get a full or partial container load?" By getting your customers to answer any of these questions, you were able to assume that they were going to buy. You then moved on to a final closing statement.

The problem with this thinking, in retail selling, is *why test the waters?* If you have opened the sale and broken resistance, effectively probed to determine what and why the customer wants the item, and made a showtime presentation of how the item will benefit the customer, have you not earned the right to close the sale?

At any time during the presentation, your customer's mind is either open or closed to making a buying decision, and I can't think of a time when it is more open to buying than after a well-executed and customized demonstration. Great salespeople assume the customer is going to buy and therefore close. This made so much sense, that "the trial close" had to become something else. It became the final close, using an add-on item as the vehicle. We will discuss the add-on part in a bit, but first let's talk about why people do not like to close.

THE DREADED CLOSE

Closing is the part of the selling process that causes most people not to want to be salespeople. The truth is that *not* being successful is the part that people don't like. If more people knew that there are more techniques to selling than being a pushy, obnoxious convincer, more people would try closing. There seem to be four types of salespeople when it comes to presentations:

1. Clerks who answer questions—if asked. No demonstrations, no relationships, no anything but being helpful—if asked. Not to worry about closing, it's not part of what they do.

2. Salespeople who make presentations with a relationship and helpfulness. But because of a personal dislike for salespeople and the desire not to be "one of the pushy types," they will leave customers to decide all by themselves after a presentation. This type is particularly helpful if the customer asks to buy.

3. The hardball closer—no relationships here. After saying hello, this type basically ask for the sale. This is the person we all dislike.

4. The professional, who takes the customers through a logical process and after doing the work, asks for the sale as a logical conclusion to a good presentation.

I, of course, prefer number 4. But I have to tell you that most of the salespeople in retail stores are number 2. And if that is the case, you would be better off being a hardball closer, because closing the sale is always better than not closing.

The Mandate

You are on the floor to sell. I can think of no other reason you were hired. Sure, you will have other duties as a part of the organization, but the truth is, selling is your major activity. It is a total invalidation of your existence to make a presentation that does not result in your asking the customer to buy. When I ran stores, not closing was the quickest and most efficient way to a new career.

The Awkwardness of Closing

Since you have to close because that is your job, you may want to consider earning the right to close so that it will be a whole lot easier. Imagine a man at a party who goes up to an attractive woman he would like to meet. He says, "I think the party is breaking up in a little while. Would you like to go to another place for drinks?" Her answer is a big "No." After a few times, he starts thinking that women today are fickle.

On the other hand, there is this approach:

A man, upon seeing a woman he is attracted to, decides he would like to meet her. He first establishes eye contact and then goes over to say hello. He chooses a simple and honest greeting line: "Hi there, I wanted to say hello and meet you. Are you enjoying the party?" She responds, "Yes." He continues with a few questions, such as, "What is your name?" and so on. He gets her to talk. He gets interested in who *she* is rather than "I'm Mack, and let me tell you about me." Things are going well, they have a drink, they are laughing. She feels comfortable enough to tell him where she works and what her hobbies are. It seems to him to be sort of magical. The party, which was an early cocktail party, breaks up about 8:00 p.m. It's still early. This is the moment of truth: he has spent the last hour and a half with this charming and attractive woman and she is about to leave. She tells him what a great time she had talking to him and gathers her coat and purse. He says, "Goodbye," and she leaves.

I don't know about you, but I have tears in my eyes relating this story. Why didn't he ask her to go out for coffee, get her telephone number or something? Maybe he didn't want to be pushy?

These two scenarios are perfect examples of the beginning of the selling process. In the second scenario he does a great job of opening and probing and demonstrates he cares. But no close.

In the first scene, he violates everything we know about the courtship dance, and he fails. In both scenes he fails. People are people and the relationship between these stories and the selling floor is all too clear.

The main difference between these stories and selling is that in selling, you had better close because it is your job. That still doesn't make it any easier to do it.

I personally have never liked the idea of coming up with a closing line. "Cash or charge?" seems terrible and out of context with my style. I have and continue to devote my selling life to the pursuit of causing the customer to say "I'll take it," rather than my having to do the asking. But again, there is no guarantee that the customer will do the asking, and it still remains my responsibility.

In doing my research, I have asked thousands of salespeople if they like to close or use closing lines. In the vast majority of cases, they say they do not. There are a truckload of books in the business section of any bookstore on the subject of closing for this very reason. But there are none on opening, probing, or the demonstration. It's no wonder that customers are apprehensive about salespeople and are frustrated by their actions.

You Have Earned the Close. Now What?

At this point you have earned the right to close and you will not be denied. But how? You certainly could use any number of techniques to close the sale, but there are some important things to consider before you ask the final closing question. And my first question is, "When are you going to add on to the primary item and build the amount of the sale?"

The Second Mandate: Adding On

The first logical question at this point is:

- Do you close the sale now and then add on, OR
- Do you add on before you close the sale on the primary item?

The answer to this question has revolutionized the way people sell and the amount of add-ons that are achieved. The answer is:

Close the Sale by Adding On!

The History of the Trial Close

In 1977, I was in the imprinted sportswear business. I had the opportunity to call on a large manufacturer of car stereos. The company was having a promotion on speakers and wanted T-shirts. I decided to come to the appointment with an idea on how they should do the shirt to promote their speaker line. I had our artist draw the oval of the speaker and put inside it the likeness of a bull dog and a little bird. The slogan on the shirt was "XYZ speakers—the best woofers and tweeters in town." I'm sure, just like you, they didn't like the idea. But an interesting thing happened. After telling me how much they didn't like it, they asked if I could get them 10,000 shirts with just their logo by next month!

A year later, I was in a welding supply store to buy some equipment (a hobby of mine at the time). I thought that as long as I was there, I might interest the owner in some imprinted shirts. I suggested he have shirts made up with the following: "Can't get your act together? Weld it," and place the company name below it. "Getting your act together" was a very 70s expression and I thought the shirt would look terrific. He didn't like the idea. He did, however, ask me if I could make him up some shirts with the company name above the breast pocket area.

In 1982, I had already formed The Friedman Group and was working in a furniture store of one of my clients, demonstrating how the selling process worked. I was showing a customer a very expensive sofa while the other salespeople were watching to see how I was going to do and placing side bets. To be frank, I was out of control. Not only did I not have enough product knowledge to make me comfortable, I had to find a way for the customer to want that sofa with that fabric instead of trying to find what she wanted in a pile of 300 swatches. I had just given her several features, advantages and benefits and got a terrific response. Out of my mouth came this line: "How about the two chairs and table that make up this group to complete your look?" She said, "No, I'll just take the sofa!"

That night, something stuck in my mind. I had made the sale by trying to make the sale larger. I recalled the T-shirt sales as being very similar. Offer this and the customer will take that. I also noted that I closed the sale without having to say "Cash or charge?" or "Would you like it shipped on Monday?" and so on. Then the research began. Presentation after presentation, I and other salespeople who learned this would add on to the sale right after the demonstration. We either sold the main item with the add-on, or sold the main item alone. Or occasionally, we would get an objection.

Adding on to close the sale makes a lot of sense for a couple of good reasons:

1. It is a soft and loving close that most salespeople can live with; and
2. You have the potential of adding on to the sale.

ADDING ON

Adding on is the second most important action salespeople take (closing is the first) when they are on the selling floor. This is true for many reasons. Here are two of the most important reasons.

126

1. On Incremental Sales, Gross Profit Equals Net Profit

Let's say your company buys an item for $50 and sells it for $100. What is left after making the sale is $50. You then subtract from the remaining $50 overhead items such as rent, salaries and commissions, telephone, insurance and so on. Maybe overhead runs at 30 percent of sales, or another $30. That leaves you with $20 profit on the $100 sale. If you sell an additional item to the same customer, you do not have to take out the overhead because it was taken out of the first item. So, all you deduct is the cost and commissions. When you sell only *one* item to a customer, you may stay in business, but when you sell additional items to each customer, you profit and your store is able to grow and prosper.

2. Good Customer Service

Several years ago, I went into a hardware store to buy a hammer. Now, I am not very mechanical, so this was going to be fun. I got into a conversation with a salesperson who showed me a $15 hammer. Wow! What is this thing going to do—do the nailing for me? I complained that $15 seemed like a lot of money for a hammer. He explained that the wood was from a certain type of tree, and the steel was this and that and that it was put together in such a way as the head wouldn't come off during hammering, so there was no safety problem.

Inside I was laughing. This guy is giving me a full-blown presentation on a hammer. I continued to complain about the $15 and he continued to convince me that I couldn't live without this "first-class" hammer. Finally, I said "Yes." Anybody who knows me will know that by him saying "first-class," I now had to have it, at any price. I got into my car, drove home with my beautiful new hammer sitting on the seat next to me, feeling very proud. I'm not sure, but I may have even actually held it up a few times for somebody to see. I got home, parked the car, put the ladder up, and got ready to do my project with . . . NO NAILS!

He took my complaining about the price as a budget problem (maybe I couldn't afford it), and to me it was a value problem (I didn't think it was worth it). I had plenty of money left to buy the nails. But in any case, isn't it good service to make sure I had all of the tools necessary to do the job?

I went to a high school reunion (here's another tear-jerker) and there she was. As beautiful as she was in high school and maybe more so. She was the one. I wanted to say hello, so I first went to the bar to get a glass of confidence. I said, "Hello," and after a few minutes of conversation, I said that I had always wished that I had asked her out in school. She said, "Why didn't you?" Ouch. Ouch.

There are lots of reasons why I didn't, but the main one was that I was afraid she would say "no." When we had this conversation ten years later, she said, "Why did you say 'no' for me?" Why indeed, I thought, and what if she had said "yes"?

The point of both of these stories is merely that if you don't ask, you will never know. And it even gets more serious if you look at it this way: who gave us the right to choose for our customers? Your obligation is to ask, not to say "yes" or "no" for your customers. We have a couple of sayings about adding on that are well worth remembering:

Ask and Ye Shall Receive
and
Show, Show, Show, Until They Say No!

Have you ever gone into a retail store, and while shopping for one particular item, spotted another you liked? And because the salesperson never got around to pulling that information out of you, you purchased only the first item?

Of course, you can't expect every customer to buy more than one item, even if you do ask all the time. But you certainly won't sell add-ons without posing the question. If every salesperson asked every customer to buy something extra every single time, add-on sales would increase and so would profits. If you take the risk that they'll say "no," you'll be surprised how many times they say "yes"!

Add-On Selling: The Golden Trial Close

Add-on selling is when the total that your customers buy is more than they intended to spend. It happens when your customer comes in for one item and you sell that item plus two others. It works when shoppers tell you they won't exceed a specific price limit, and by the time they leave your store, they have spent double. Add-on selling can be a thoroughly enjoyable way to do business, because it can be lots of fun.

The Golden Trial Close is intended primarily to help you move into the close on the major item; there's no point in your being on the floor if you aren't closing sales. However, the technique also gives you opportunities to increase the number of sales you make and the profits you reap. The result is synergism, because adding on gives you the opportunity to sell multiple items to one customer. It is called "golden" because it turns the trial close to gold.

The Buying Room

Let's say a shopper comes in to buy a suit. He makes it clear that the maximum he wants to spend is $400, but he has his eye on a garment that costs $550 and it's driving him crazy. The customer tries on the more expensive suit and it looks like it was custom-made for him. The customer feels good, he looks great, and it's clear he won't be able to resist the higher-priced suit. You can see that he's decided that he *has* to have that suit.

He comes out of the dressing room and finds you standing near the register to tell you he'll take the $550 suit. Is this the time to add on? Or, do you feel sorry for him because he's spending $150 more than he told you he wanted to spend originally?

No, it isn't time to add on, because a fascinating mental process takes place after a customer decides to buy. Let's say you're looking at that same $550 suit and it's more money than you've ever spent on a suit in your entire life. After hemming and hawing in the dressing room, looking at yourself in the mirror from all angles, you finally say, "Ah, what the heck, I'll do it." At that exact moment, do you, a) think about all the other things you need to buy to go along with the suit, or, b) wonder how long it will take for the tailoring to be completed, how you'll look at the interview for which you purchased the suit, or how you can't wait to get the suit home to show your girlfriend. I think you'll agree that choice 'b' is the one we can best relate to. My experience tells me that the last thing he'd consider at this point is spending more money.

The best time to attempt the add-on is right after or during the demonstration. You've gone through all the steps leading up to the demonstration and you've done a spectacular presentation. Your customer has been receptive and you feel confident that he will make the main purchase. While the wheels are turning in the customer's mind and enthusiasm to buy is at its peak, *that* is the time to add on.

Adding on Before He Makes the Big Decision

Let's stay with our customer and his $550 suit. He has taken the garment into the dressing room to try it on. Although he said the suit was out of his price range, he didn't say that he couldn't afford it, only that he didn't want to spend that much money on a suit. Nevertheless, you can see that he is impressed by its cut, the feel of the material, the superior workmanship you have demonstrated to match the needs you uncovered during probing.

He's envisioning ownership and teetering on the brink, so while he's in the dressing room you take the bull by the horns. You collect shirts, ties, socks, and pocket squares that perfectly match "his" suit. When he emerges from the dressing room, or better yet, even while he's still in there, you suggest to him, "How about this perfectly-matched tie and pocket square to complete the look of your new suit?"

Have you said anything about buying the suit? No, and it's not necessary because you're working on the assumption that the suit is as good as sold. In fact, during the opening, probing and demonstration you haven't asked the customer to do anything. Now you have an unspoken expectation that the customer will be doing something, and that something is to buy the suit.

The Trial Close

The trial close is one simple question that closes the sale on the main item and adds on as well. It is a low-key, customer-oriented question, designed to keep you directly involved with that particular customer and his or her needs. Offering your expertise in this way does two important things: it facilities the purchase of the item, and it enhances your service to the customer by providing everything the customer needs.

Nearly everyone can relate to a closing situation with a customer when there is an uncomfortable pause. You've been through the entire selling process; you've pointed out all of the benefits of the item you are demonstrating; and you've matched the item to the customer's needs. You thought things were going well, yet nothing seems to be happening. This is the dreadful moment in the process, the terrible lull when the salesperson needs to be asking the customer to buy. You can't simply hope or wish real hard that the customer will say, "I'll take it."

What happens now is the trial close. It is your chance to fulfill your mandates: to close the sale and add on. Your simple question has to contain language that *simultaneously ties the add-on to the main item and the customer's ownership to the merchandise.* In our example we used the words "your new suit" to accomplish this objective. These words give the customer automatic ownership of the main item, the suit, and presents an opportunity for the customer to consider the purchase of the accessories that will give the suit a finished appearance.

Heap It On!

Whenever you trial close by adding on, heap it on. It's a simple theory that works. I can't remember who told me this story, but it was brilliant. It's about an egg salesperson who was calling on a free-standing hamburger stand. The egg salesperson asked the owner if he'd sold very many eggs to go in people's milkshakes. The answer was no. The salesperson pointed out that the price of a milkshake made with eggs is higher than a milkshake made without eggs.

131

If the customer says, "I want a chocolate milkshake," he suggested the owner say, "Would you prefer one egg or two?" I think you know the result: there were lots of eggs sold in shakes.

While working with clients recently in Australia, who sold mostly electronics, I suggested they could double their battery sales by pulling out a four- or eight-pack of expensive alkaline batteries and saying to the customer, "I recommend these." It puts the burden on the customer to say no. Also, it seems as though when offering customers six items, they take four; if you offer them four items, they take two; if you offer them two items, they take one. It's incredible how many times when customers are offered additional items, they wind up with some of them. Every time the customer purchases additional items, the store profits and your commissions increase.

CONSTRUCTING A TRIAL CLOSE

Here is the five-step process to heap it on and secure additional sales for yourself. The steps are easy to learn and will help you have fun closing the sale.

1   2   3

"[How about] this [perfectly matched] [tie and pocket square]

4   5

[to complete the look] of [your] new suit?"

Step One: **"HOW ABOUT"**	**"How about . . ."** Starting with these words ensures that your TRIAL CLOSE will be phrased as a question. Far from being pushy, this way of starting the trial close begins with two completely unassuming words and sounds like a friendly, discovery question.
Step Two: **"THE ENHANCER"**	**"this perfectly matched . . ."** Before you state the add-on itself, no mere mention of it will do. Be creative, paint a word picture. Speak of the add-on as something that enhances the main

item, something that is functional, special, or necessary, and falls within the framework of your customer's stated needs. Consider the difference between saying, "Do you want anything for dessert?" versus "We have some hot apple pie that's absolutely sensational."

Step Three: "THE ADD-ON"	**"tie and pocket square . . ."** Suppose that during probing you learned that the customer who came in for the suit is going to wear it for an important interview, so you have carefully chosen the accessories that you suggest as add-ons. You don't recommend any old tie and pocket square; you offer finely made accessories that are perfectly matched to that outstanding suit.
Step Four: "MUST HAVE"	**"to complete the look . . ."** This is a word or phrase that encourages the customer to feel as though the add-on is absolutely essential to the main purchase. If we say that the accessories "will complete the look" of the suit, it suggests that, although the suit is handsome and looks splendid on the customer, the image created will be incomplete without the addition of the accessories. It makes your customers feel that they "must have" the add-ons.
Step Five: "POSSESSION"	**"of your new suit."** Adding the word "you" or "your" ties customers to the main items by giving them automatic possession of it, and also gives customers the opportunity to see how the accessory items add value to "their" new merchandise.

This technique is a far cry from "Will there be anything else?" and "Would you like a new tie, also?" Those tired lines are ready for retirement. You don't have to be embarrassed by them, and your customers don't have to be put to sleep by them anymore. The trial close is such a simple and effective method, and requires so little training, that it's fascinating how few salespeople ever use it.

They Won't Buy If You Won't Sell

Several years ago, a group of volunteers were sent out with American Express Gold Cards and told to buy, buy, buy. There was no ceiling on the amount of money they could spend; the only limitation was that the customers had to stop buying when the salespeople stopped selling.

Not surprisingly, very little money was charged against the credit cards in that experiment. The results: 60 percent of the salespeople went for a second item, 25 percent went on for a third item, and only 5 percent asked for a fourth item. And the most significant statistic of them all, only about 1 percent went for a fifth or more.

In another study, conducted at a famous university, 20 students were sent out to a shopping mall, each with $100. They were instructed to go into a store and buy something inexpensive. If the salesperson tried to sell something additional, they were to purchase it. Thereafter, they were to continue buying everything suggested by the salesperson until the suggestions stopped or the money ran out. All of the students came back with change.

When do your knees start to shake? At $500, $1,000, $5,000? Remember, it's a combination of taste level and what your customers can afford to spend that determines how far you can go. And you'll never be rich with commissions if you're afraid to ask.

Salespeople have only two choices: either they make the sale and attempt an add-on, or they stop calling themselves salespeople. It's hard to do at first, and it's a rare salesperson who can include all five parts of the question every single time. As long as you get the idea and get close, it's perfectly acceptable. It's not always easy to think on our feet and sound spontaneous about what we're saying.

Practice helps this immensely. Remember, your customers won't continue to buy, buy, buy if you don't continue to sell, sell, sell.

Staying in Control

When you use the trial close, you put yourself in charge of the transaction. You are the one who determines the direction of what remains of the presentation. You know what ground you've covered, where you want to go next, and how to get there. *You are in control,* and the certainty that you have will give you the confidence you need to complete the sale.

One of the ways you stay in control is by realizing that there are only three responses you can get to the Trial Close:

1. The customer will buy only the main item.
2. The customer will buy the main item and an add-on item.
3. The customer will raise an objection to buying the main item.

If your customers have committed to the main item and have agreed to buy an add-on, not only do you win, you win double. Bingo! If your customers say they would like to see the suggested add-on, you can assume they have agreed to buy the main item.

Even if they object to seeing the additional item, you can still assume that they have agreed to buy the main item. Bingo! Otherwise, they would have said "no" to the main item as well.

In either of the first two cases, you have made the sale. *You are in control,* because you made it happen.

Even in the third case, if the customer objects to buying the main item, you are still in a better position than you might think. Your customer may say something like, "I think I want to shop around a little more," or "The price is too high," or "I want to think it over." Salespeople hear objections like these all the time (covered in detail in the next chapter), and the customer can voice them at any point during your presentation.

If you're not prepared to deal with objections when the customer states them, you will be caught off-guard. However, during the trial close you are *looking* for objections, because the sale can't be closed if obstacles remain. When you learn to engineer the process so that customers voice their objections when you're ready to hear them, *you remain in control.*

Selling Non-Companion Add-Ons

As you gain more experience using the trial close, you may wish to offer as add-ons articles that are not companion pieces to the main item. Perhaps the customer said something during probing that leads you in another direction entirely. Before you add on an unrelated item, remove the primary item you sold from the scene.

Tell the customer that you're going to "just leave this up at the register," and put the primary item out of sight. By permitting you to do that, the customer gives further commitment for the purchase of the main item, and implies approval of your assumption that you have made the sale. Once the main article is out of sight, you can focus attention on the add-on without risking that the customer will feel overwhelmed. If the article is too big to physically move to the register, removing the label or price tag and writing the SKU on an order form or something similar will do.

Practice, Practice, Practice

The only way to feel comfortable using the trial close is to practice doing it. The phrasing has to be kept uncomplicated, using simple, conversational language so you don't trip over the words. It can be used with any item you sell in your store. Here are a few examples in different industries to give you an idea of how they sound:

- "How about a lightweight racquet for your wife, too, so she'll have an equal chance when you use *your* new racquet?"

- "How about these easy-to-use drill attachments to make it simple to install your new front door?"

- "How about this fashionable tennis bracelet to enhance the look of your new watch?"
- "How about this specially-formulated leather treatment kit to protect your new briefcase?"
- "How about a convenient thermal lid to make it easy to cover and uncover your new spa?"
- "How about a waterproof doghouse to protect your new puppy from the rain?"
- "How about a convenient carrying case to safeguard your new CD player from unexpected bumps?"

The Inexpensive Option

Until you've incorporated the trial close into your professional performance and adapted it to your own style, you may want to consider offering inexpensive add-ons. This way you can slowly work your way up to higher-priced merchandise. Begin by suggesting small items. If they don't work, not much has been risked and your self-confidence won't be undermined. Here are some examples:

- "How about this specially formulated shoe care to help protect your new shoes?"
- "How about a coordinating dust ruffle to accent your comforter and create the look you wanted to achieve?"

As you become more proficient, you will learn that add-ons don't have to be less expensive than the main item. People don't always "lump together" different categories of purchases. For example, for many customers, clothing and shoes are on separate budgets. When customers buy jewelry, it may have nothing to do with the crystal they want to put on display in their china hutch. Yet in both cases, each unrelated item may be found in the same store.

When you have developed your skills, you may want to try add-ons that have nothing to do with the primary purchase, or even with what you have uncovered during probing. Your growing competence and your resulting self-confidence will help you "know" what kind of add-on to suggest to any customer coming into your store. It may seem far-fetched now, but it *will become almost instinctive* to know when you can offer a piece of giftware to a customer who is buying a watch. And you haven't lived until you've sold the customer a $15 kickstand and added on a $2,000 bicycle to go on top of it!

Whether the add-on item requires the presence of the main item or not, remember that you are in control. You conducted the sales process in a way that caused the customer to commit to the main item. You managed the trial close so that the customer agreed to consider an add-on. There is no reason why you can't keep adding on a third, fourth, or even fifth item.

While the trial close won't get every customer to purchase add-on items every time, it's still the easiest and simplest way to sell the main item. If you say, "How about a specially designed cover to protect your new racquet?" and the customer says, "No, I'll just take the racquet," you've made the sale. Bingo!

If the customer says, "Yes, let me take a look at the racquet cover," you're on your way to selling an add-on. Bingo! If the customer takes the racquet and buys the cover, what's to stop you from saying, "How about this perfectly coordinated tennis outfit to make you look like a pro with your brand new racquet?" Bingo!

Show, Show, Show,
Until They Say No!

HOT TIPS AND KEY INSIGHTS

- The dislike of closing is a direct result of the old and hackneyed methods that salespeople use in selling.
- The conventional trial close is boring to the salesperson and to the customer as well. There is no need for the traditional trial close, which is intended to determine if the customer will make a commitment to a particular purchase.
- If you've done a good job with the up-front work for the sale, the customer will be ready to buy and you can proceed directly from showtime to add-on time.

- On incremental sales, gross profit virtually equals net profit.

- It is the professional salesperson's mandate to close the sale and attempt an add-on every single time with every single customer.

- The Golden Trial Close, which got its name because it results in almost sure profit, eliminates negative feelings about closing.

- The trial close employs a simple five-part question that can be phrased easily and spontaneously. Its components are: the *How about...* beginning, the *enhancer*, the name of the add-on, the *must have*, and the addition of the possessive word *you* or *your*.

- To be effective, use the trial close immediately after the demonstration, when you feel comfortable in assuming that your customer will buy the main item.

- When you use the Golden Trial Close, you put yourself in charge of the transaction. You are the one who determines the direction of what remains of the presentation.

- There are only three responses you can get to the Golden Trial Close: the customer will buy only the main item; the customer will buy the main item and an add-on item; the customer will raise an objection to buying the main item.

- If your customers say they would like to see the suggested add-on, you can assume they have agreed to buy the main item. If they object to seeing the additional item, you can still assume that they have agreed to buy the main item.

- As you gain more expertise using the trial close, offer articles as add-ons that are not companion pieces to the main item. Wait until you are comfortable in assuming that the customer will buy the primary merchandise. Then remove the "sold" article from the scene.

- Whether the add-on item requires the presence of the main item or not, remember that you are in control.

There is no reason why you can't keep adding on—a third, fourth or even fifth item.

- While the trial close won't get every customer to purchase add-on items every time, it's almost guaranteed to sell at least the main item.

- Until you've incorporated the trial close and adapted it to your own style, consider offering inexpensive add-ons to slowly work your way up to higher-priced merchandise.

- As you become more proficient, you will learn that add-ons don't have to cost less than the main item. Also, try add-ons that have nothing to do with the primary purchases. Your growing competence and self-confidence will help you to "know" what kind of add-on to suggest to any customer coming into your store.

- Remember the salesperson's "Rap"—Show, Show, Show, Until They Say No!

CHAPTER SIX

HANDLING OBJECTIONS

If I were to create an ideal scenario, you'd be reading this chapter for fun, not purpose.

You have completed the trial close and:

- You know how to go directly from showtime to add-on time;
- Your trial close keeps you in control; and
- You Show, Show, Show—Until They Say No!

Many salespeople still interpret a customer's objection as a "no sale." We think that an unwillingness to buy now means that the customer has rejected the merchandise and spurned us. In fact, customers started objecting as soon as the first salesperson ever started selling, and for as many reasons as there are stars in the sky.

Objections are a big part of the retail game, but they don't have to mean you've lost the sale.

Customer objections, unless they are handled perceptively, with tact and finesse, will keep you from doing what you want to do: make the sale. This book is devoted entirely to teaching the process for successful retail selling. Each and every step in the process is vital. But this chapter should be the least significant of them all if you have opened, probed and demonstrated well. But if you haven't, this chapter may be the most significant of them all. If you paid close attention to the previous chapters, it's time to get out your magnifying glass for this one.

The Trial of Trial and Error

Retail selling has a long history; people have been engaged in it since the first marketplace opened thousands of years ago. All salespeople have somehow personalized the process of selling by adapting their individual skills and personalities to relate to the customer. Through trial and error, some figure out what works. Some never do. The cost of trial and error, however, is way too expensive today.

Suppose there are 500 people on an island, completely cut off from civilization. One person becomes ill and suddenly there's a need for someone to assume the role of doctor. Someone volunteers to take on this assignment. The patient leans over and says, "I've got a terrible pain in my side." The doctor-person smacks the patient on his side and the patient dies. The "doctor" makes a note in his book not to do that anymore when a patient complains of a side pain (good move!).

Over the years, the "doctor" sees many more patients with many different illnesses and tries many different methods to cure them. As he attempts to unravel the mysteries of medicine through trial and error, many of his patients die. Each time, he makes a note in his book.

One day, someone comes in with a similar pain in the side and the "doctor" operates to remove a little inflamed object from inside the patient. Wonder of wonders, the patient lives, and the "doctor" writes this in his book.

Eventually, the "doctor" dies and someone else offers to assume the role of "doctor." The new "doctor" then has two choices: start from scratch using trial-and-error experi-

142

ments on everyone who comes in with a complaint, or read the other "doctor's" book.

To save you time, I'm going to lay out a precise formula that will get you past objections and to the cash register with more regularity. Never mind that you'll be following someone else's plan. You want economic results, not intellectual property rights. It's not necessary to reinvent the wheel every time you need something that's round. If humans had to learn everything in life by trial and error, we wouldn't learn much.

Some people, nevertheless, refuse to read "the book." If they do read it, they resist using what they learn from it, or they allow themselves to fall back into familiar, although unproductive, routines. The techniques presented in *this* book and in this chapter in particular, are the result of an intensive study of what great salespeople in our society have done, from retailers to wholesalers, from sellers of religious ideas to sellers of philosophy.

All of these sales leaders have something to contribute to the way we conduct ourselves in our retail stores. Their accomplishments and experience have been distilled here into the precise formula that will work in handling customer objections. Study this chapter and learn to use the formula. In some cases, use it *verbatim*, as it is written. Then surely there will be no need to reinvent the wheel.

WHY OBJECTIONS OCCUR

If ever there was a part of the selling process that is steeped in myth, it's the one that deals with handling objections. It is also the step that salespeople most often violate. Remember, the bottom line is that most of the time people buy for two reasons: trust and value. If those are the reasons your customers *do* buy, it follows that the reasons they don't buy are a *lack* of trust or value.

It's a bonus if the customer trusts you as a salesperson, but as we discussed in the demonstration, it won't help with the sale if the value of the merchandise has not been established. Similarly, it is difficult to close the sale if the customer feels no trust in you. Either way, you're going to get an objection, although it's easier to surmount the problem of the product's perceived value than it is to overcome lack of trust in you.

You Didn't Do Enough

If shoppers aren't buying because they think the item lacks value, they're letting you know that they haven't had their needs or desires met. They haven't been persuaded or been offered good enough reasons to make a positive decision about the merchandise today. If customers aren't buying because they don't like you, then you probably have not done a good job of establishing empathy and trust, or even moved past resistance.

Most of the time when customers object, they give you a false or incomplete reason for not buying. They find it difficult to come right out and say what's wrong, so they use stock phrases to avoid saying what is on their minds:

"I'll be back."
"I want to shop around."
"Can you hold this for me?"
"I'm not sure; I really should bring my wife in with me."

These kinds of objections are called "stalls," and they're used when customers feel uncomfortable or embarrassed about telling you the real reasons for their objection.

Many customers may have difficulty stating their true feelings no matter how well or how poorly you have done your job. Ironically, the better you are at building trust with customers, particularly during the probing process, the more difficult it may be for them to state their actual objections. They may feel almost guilty about saying no to the purchase because you *have* established empathy and they don't want to disappoint a new friend.

Conversely, if you have done a poor job of building trust, the customer's objection is likely to be more strongly felt, and the customer will find any excuse to leave the store. When customers lack trust in the salesperson, even if it is possible to uncover their real objections, it is usually more difficult to overcome their buying hesitation. Customers who don't trust you will resent your trying to handle their objections in any way.

Better Shop Around

Have Mr. and Mrs. "Be-Back" been to your store? You remember them. They liked the crystal you demonstrated to them, and they'll "be back." They're going to return (it's a sure thing) with "Mr. Look-Around." He thinks you have a terrific selection of fine quality briefcases, but he needs to "look around."

Sometimes a customer's hesitation to purchase the item is a defense mechanism to delay making a decision. It's not easy for any of us to part with our money, so why should it be any easier for our customers? I can remember falling in love with a beautiful and very expensive watch when I was working with a jewelry client. Now, watches happen to be a bit of an obsession of mine. I just like them. At the time, I think I had about 16 in my collection, but this particular watch was the pièce de résistance. I wanted it in a big way and I knew I could rationalize its purchase. But I still had to try it on every month when I visited the client for three consecutive months before finally making the decision. As I was fondling it again and expressing how much I wanted that watch, the owner of the store said, "You don't really want it." I said, "What do you mean? Of course I do." He said, "Well, if you really wanted it, it would be yours already." That did it. I had the jeweler size it immediately and wore it home.

There are also a large number of people in this world who just can't make a decision. The husband of one of my employees is a perfect example. He's always the last one to place his order at a restaurant because he never can decide what to have. We've all met this type: can't decide what movie to go see, can't decide where to eat, what to eat, what to drink, what to wear in the morning, what to buy someone as a gift, etc. Nevertheless, the vast majority of customer objections exist because of what the salesperson has done, or not done, in the sales process.

Many customers do want to shop around before making a decision. When you hear, "I want to shop around," though, you have no way of knowing whether they mean it, or whether they have already shopped everywhere else. They may be accustomed to using that stock phrase to get out of the stores they visit, and they may be doing to you what they did to other salespeople before they saw you.

Alternatively, customers may fib a little bit by saying, "I want to shop around," or "I want to think it over," when it could have been that the item is too expensive. In that case, you can spend all day trying to overcome "I want to shop around," and because it's not the real problem, you'll never close the sale. That's why it's vital for you to work towards uncovering the real objection and not simply taking the customer's statement at face value.

Everybody Fibs

We all have fibbed a little and said we'd be back when we had no intention of coming back. We've all said it was the wrong color when it was really the price. Some of us have gone to extremes to make sure the salesperson wasn't disappointed by saying things like, "What time do you close?" or "Do you work tomorrow?", all methods of keeping the salesperson's hopes alive even though there is no intention of returning. And some of us even promised we'd come back with our spouse when we didn't *have* one. These are things that happen every day on the selling floor. Yet, when customers do them to us, our tendency is to believe them. If *we* do it to salespeople when we go shopping, there's a 100 percent chance that customers do it to us.

Assuming you're past probing, the demonstration and the trial close, some of the real reasons customers may object to buying are because they feel that the item:

- May be obsolete as soon as technology progresses;
- Can't be justified because it's more than they need;
- Isn't worth the price, even though they like it;
- Costs more than they can spend; or
- Doesn't have all of the features they need or want.

Maybe They Don't Know

Frequently, customers aren't sure what they want, and they can't clearly communicate to you what they don't know themselves. If a customer says the china isn't elegant enough, find a more elegant pattern. You may have to do this several times during a presentation, until you hit on something that catches the customer's eye. It's your job to satisfy the customer's wants, even when customers don't know for sure what they want. Remember to keep your enthusiasm level high throughout the process, and to avoid showing frustration at the customers' inability to explain what they want.

Whether customers are unable to state the real reason for not buying, or whether they just don't know what they want, there's no way to handle customer objections unless we can define them. We have to be diligent, but not pushy about getting our customers to tell us why they are hesitating about the purchase. Until we know how they actually feel about the merchandise, we are showing that we cannot complete the sale.

WORK WITH THE CUSTOMER

It seems like some aggressive salespeople think that overcoming customer objections means arguing with customers, or wearing them down until they buy. Some sales trainers even suggest you ignore objections and continue closing. On the other hand, many salespeople are so concerned about sounding pushy that it is out of the question to try and uncover objections, much less to deal with them.

Successfully overcoming objections depends almost entirely on the salesperson's ability to work *with* the customer. It means having complete empathy with the customer's feelings, and the ability to put yourself in the customer's shoes. It also means you do not create an "us versus them" situation by presenting the store against the customer. On the contrary, you have to put yourself on the customers' side by being sensitive to their concerns.

It's a rare customer who spends $5,000 with ease the first time he or she walks into a store. It has happened, but you can understand that most people actually want to think about a major purchase before they make a commitment to it. In some cases, spending $50 or even $25 causes concern.

I'll never forget one of the most humbling experiences of my life. I was ringing up the final payment on a gold chain a woman had put on layaway. It was undoubtedly the thinnest gold chain on the planet. I mean if you blew on it, it might break. It was 14 karat gold and retailed at $24! But this woman was so excited about picking it up that it might as well have cost $10,000. She said it was the most expensive present she had ever bought for her husband. Whoa! Here I am thinking it's the cheapest hunk of junk ever made and she's going to proudly present it to her husband. It's a good thing that I wasn't the original person to sell it to her, or I would have been likely to try and sell her a much more masculine, heavy chain, whose price would have blown her out of the store and into the underwear department at Sears.

If you can appreciate your customers' position on price, say so. If they say the price is too high, give some understanding to their feelings. Let your customers know that you care about their concerns.

After years in development, this chapter is devoted to teaching the precise method for properly handling customer objections. Unlike the approaches for dealing with other parts of the sales process, *this prescription needs to be followed as closely as possible.* This six-step procedure can be used to deal with virtually any customer objection, and does so in a way that lets the customer feel your support and appreciate your concern.

Step One: Listen to the Entire Objection. Don't interrupt customers in mid-sentence, as that implies what they have to say is not important enough to hear. If you let them finish voicing their concerns, you may discover they were just moaning a little before making a commitment to the purchase.

Customer: Boy, it really is expensive.
(Salesperson waits a couple of seconds before saying anything.)
Customer: Oh . . . I'm going to go ahead and take it.

148

Who knows? It's possible!

Step Two: Acknowledge the Objection. Can you understand or appreciate that customers may want to look around, or they feel the price is too high, or they want to talk to their spouse? Your customers will be absolutely delighted to know that you can share their concern. By restating the objection verbatim, preceded by "I can understand . . ." or "I can appreciate . . ." you put yourself on the customer's side. To further confirm your understanding and empathy, pose a grabber after the acknowledgement.

Objection:	I'll be back.
Acknowledgement:	I can understand that you'd like to come back later. It's an important decision and you want to make the right choice, don't you?
Objection:	I need to talk to my husband (wife) first.
Acknowledgement:	I can appreciate that you want to talk to your husband first. You want to make sure that both of you are happy with your selection, right?
Objection:	I really should go home and measure first.
Acknowledgement:	I can understand that you feel you need to measure first. You certainly want to make sure it will fit perfectly, don't you?

Step Three: Getting Permission to Continue. Prior to asking your customer any further questions, I find it most polite to seek permission by asking, "May I ask you a question?" In a sense, you're getting their permission to continue the dialogue.

Step Four: Do You Like It? You may need to ask several questions to uncover the true objection, but the first question is always, "Do you like the item?" Such a direct question often encourages customers to open up and tell you exactly what's on their mind.

Step Five: The Smoke-Out. During the demo, you presented features, advantages and benefits of the product. In this step, you reconfirm your selling points to see if the customers are still in agreement that it's what they wanted.

Step Six: Ask the Customer About Price. Always ask this question last after nothing else has turned up and phrase it in a non-threatening way: "How do you feel about the price?"

The example below will give you an idea of how steps two, three and four sound in a conversation. Note how the flow of the process puts you "in sync" with what's going on for the customer. Keep in mind the importance of appearing empathetic to the customer while speaking from this "script"; a little rehearsal will make your performance Academy Award quality.

Objection:	I'd like to talk it over with my husband.
Acknowledgement and Grabber:	I certainly can appreciate that. It's important that both of you like what you're getting. You both want to be delighted with this purchase, don't you?
Response:	Oh, yes.
Permission to ask a question:	But before you go, may I ask you a question?
Broad-Based Question:	Do you like it?

When hearing any number of objections, many salespeople just fold up and hand over their business card. Then they'll say, "Ask for me. I'm here every day but Wednesday." If you just give out your card and let these potential customers go, they're unlikely to come back. Or, if they do come back, it will probably be on Wednesday, the one day you're not there.

Some salespeople may feel angry and become argumentative when customers say they have to consult their husbands or wives or shop around or go home and measure. They want to say, "Don't you ever decide on anything by yourself?" Instead they say, "Our prices are the most competitive in town. Why don't I just write it up for you and you can take it home to your wife." The salesperson who displays anger or frustration will simply stimulate the same feelings in the customer.

Acknowledging the customer's feelings encourages the customer to appreciate that you are an empathetic person. However, you want to be cautious not to cross the fine line between *acknowledging* the customer's objections and *agreeing* with the customer's reason for not buying. You don't want to find yourself saying, "You're right, you should shop around first," or "I agree, this one is too expensive."

> *You want to understand your customer's feelings, but you don't want to endorse them.*

So far, we have acknowledged the objection, asked permission to ask a question, and then asked, "Do you like it?" The customer who replies, "Yes, I like it," is performing a self-reinforcing task that is another step toward the purchase. If customers say they do not like the item, or say they do but they're not very convincing, find out what they don't like and fix it.

Suppose in answer to the question, "Do you like the strand?" the customer said, "Oh, it's all right." This is a real danger signal, a red flag to warn you that what's happening is hazardous to your sale.

If the customer is giving a "just okay" or even a casual "yes" response, either you missed something important during probing or the customer doesn't know what he or she wants. *If you want to salvage the sale, you have to probe again to discover what you missed,* or to help the customers clarify their needs through the process of trial and error.

You've got two choices: proceed to the smoke-out or take advantage of a great opportunity to shorten the whole process. When I hear "It's all right," or "It's okay," I counter immediately with, "Now wait a minute. I don't sell 'just okay' merchandise. Tell me what the problem is." Said with a lot of love and a twinkle in the eye, it works for me 9 out of 10 times and the customer spills the beans with no further questions. But if it doesn't work, the smoke-out is the next best strategy.

THE SMOKE-OUT

During probing, you determined the personal reasons your customers wanted the item: it's to be given as a gift, they've always wanted one, their neighbor has one, etc. You've used all this information when you presented Feature-Advantage-Benefit-Grabbers, and you were careful to match the merchandise to the customer's needs.

We have already noted that the customers who object to the merchandise find it difficult to say what's on their minds, and the reasons they give are almost always excuses. Now we have to detect what's bothering them. We have to find out if the benefits we demonstrated, the ones they said they wanted, were really what they were after. To do this, we have to review the Feature-Advantage-Benefit-Grabbers, and encourage the customers into letting us "smoke out" the truth.

Suppose you are in your store showing a leather chair to a customer. Based on the information the customer gave you during probing, you chose to emphasize two Feature-Advantage-Benefit-Grabbers. The first is that the style was traditional and would look good with everything in her house. The second is that the cushions were filled with goose down, which makes it incredibly comfortable.

Trial Close

Salesperson: How about this perfectly matched ottoman to put your feet on while you relax in your new chair?

Objection

Customer: You know, I really think I should think about it for a while.

Agreement and Grabber

Salesperson: I can really understand you wanting to think about it. When you select a a beautiful piece of furniture for your home, you want to make sure you're making the right decision, don't you?

Response

Customer: Yes, I sure do.

Permission to Ask a Question

Salesperson: May I ask you a question?

Customer: Sure.

Smoke-Out Question

Salesperson: Do you like the chair?

Answer

Customer: It's lovely.

Support

Salesperson: Yes, it's gorgeous, isn't it? Finding a chair that's as comfortable as you said it was is very special.

Smoke-Out Question

Salesperson: Let me ask you this, how did you feel about the traditional style?

Answer

Customer: Oh, I think it'll fit right in.

Support

Salesperson: Based on what you told me about the other furniture in your home, I thought this would be a perfect match.

Smoke-Out Question

Salesperson: How did you feel about the down cushions?

Answer

Customer: Well, actually, I was a little concerned about my son's allergies.

There it is at last! The objection never was that she wanted to "think it over," and as we re-examined the benefits, we found out what was really bothering her. This is a typical customer reaction; for some reason, she couldn't speak truthfully about the real issue on her mind until you sought it out. However, once you identified the down filling as a source of the customer's objection, you can ask follow-up questions to learn what the problem is or as we say "fix it." Then you can demonstrate other cushion fillings that will work for her.

Resist offering layaway and credit plans during this stage of overcoming objections, because you don't yet know whether the problem is budget. If your customers aren't happy with the item, it won't matter that you're competitive, or that it's the last one in stock, or that they can pay for it in installments. Let's see how things could have gone wrong on the last example:

Trial Close: How about this perfectly matched ottoman to put your feet on while you relax in your new chair?

Objection: You know, I really think I should think about it for a while.

Salesperson: Well, why don't you go ahead and put it on layaway so you make sure you can get it. This floor model is the last one we have in stock.

Customer: Oh, I don't think so. I'll be able to make a decision by tomorrow morning. I really just have to sleep on it.

And off she goes to another store to find a chair without down cushions.

If a customer ever objects to a particular feature of the article you are demonstrating, it is often the result of poor communication during the probing process. For example, your customers' specific objections might be that they don't like the shape of the stone in a ring, or the carpet isn't the right color, or the shoes aren't formal enough for what they had in mind. If you can get accurate information from probing, you won't have to waste energy showing merchandise your customers don't like.

If you're ever going to find out what's going on in the customer's mind, the time is now. Unless you can expose the real objection and overcome it, the method of payment is never going to be a solution.

HANDLING THE PRICE OBJECTION

It's important to smoke out any potential obstacles that might exist prior to raising the issue of price. If your customers' only concern is how a particular feature may benefit them, you can fix those problems and never have to ask about the price. The cost of the item is best raised last, after you are sure there is no other issue.

Smoke out each FABG you gave in the demo and then bring up the price. Because customers are frequently reluctant, and sometimes even embarrassed, to talk freely about money, your question needs to be phrased in a non-threatening way:

"How did you feel about the price?"

The response will either be that it's too high, or it's fine; no one ever complains that the price is too low. If the price is fine and you have a trusting relationship with the customer, then it has to be that the value is lacking. Acknowledge the customer's feelings by stating that you appreciate her concern about the price. Explain that your merchandise is a great value and it's important to you that your customers understand that. Then it's time to pull out your cannon.

Salesperson: How do you feel about the price?

Customer: Oh, it's fine.

Salesperson: I'm glad you said that. We really take a lot of pride in our pricing. We make sure that customers get terrific value for their hard-earned money.

Salesperson: You know, I'm sorry, but I forgot to tell you something about these pearls that makes them unique. If you look closely you'll see they have a thick nacre. When they put the nucleus in the oyster to make the cultured pearl, the oyster releases a secretion around it.

In time, this becomes nacre, the coating which lends lustre to the pearl. These pearls are almost translucent. Isn't the color lovely? That doesn't happen all of the time, because we can't control the development of the nacre even when we give the pearl its start.

The salesperson has given the customer additional information and has also shown expertise about the merchandise. The salesperson probably didn't use a lot of product knowledge earlier because he didn't need it. He was just trying to get the customer to fall in love with the pearls, and didn't overuse technical words to accomplish that. Later, in dealing with an objection, it's perfectly alright to show how much you know about your merchandise. In this way, you can give customers additional reasons to trust you and additional value to the product.

As we saw in Chapter 5, saving information for use later in the sale is an important concept. If you tell your customer everything you know at the beginning of the process, what will you do later if you have to add value? Remember to keep some material in reserve for later use as ammunition. Don't use all your cannons early on; it will be anticlimactic if you have to use a BB gun to overcome objections later.

Is It Value or Budget?

If customers tell you that the price is too high, you need to figure out whether they are talking about budget or value. You may remember, in the last chapter, when I was in the hardware store I was upset about the $15 cost of a hammer. The question is whether I was saying I couldn't *afford* the hammer, or whether I thought it wasn't *worth spending* $15 for a hammer. If I couldn't afford it, the salesperson was dealing with a budget consideration; if I thought the hammer wasn't worth it, the salesperson had to overcome a concern about value.

If the customer buying the pearls objects to their high price, acknowledge her feelings this way: "I can certainly understand your concerns about the price. Things are expensive today, aren't they?" Notice the use of the word "things," and that you do not name any item specifically, especially not the merchandise under consideration. Also note another grabber, reminding her once again that I am on her side. The salesperson continues:

> *"Is the price of this particular item too high, or is it just more than you wanted to spend today?"*

If the customer's problem is that the price of the article is too high, acknowledge again that you can appreciate the customer's concern, and then add Big Bertha, the biggest cannon of all time:

> *An interesting thing about pearls is that Mother Nature controls them, even though we put in the nucleus ourselves. So we can't be sure of getting enough quality pearls for a matched strand of this size and color. It takes a great deal of time to create a strand that looks as great as these do on you; that's why they seem to be so expensive. But that's a small price to pay for something that you'll have and love for so many years to come. I think that's an important consideration, don't you?*

Observe that we have offered another Feature-Advantage-Benefit-Grabber every time we uncover an objection for which lack of value is the underlying reason.

If your customer's objection is that the item costs more than he or she wanted to spend today, acknowledge again that you understand how the customer feels and ask:

> *"How much did you want to spend today?"*

Note the use of the word "today," which reinforces that you are talking about now rather than later.

Notice also that, until this part of the process, you have not asked the dreaded "How much" question: "How much did you want to spend?" You certainly avoided asking that question when the customer first came in, because you didn't want to be bound by an unrealistic price the customer may have had in mind. After all, each one of us has spent more in retail stores than we originally planned to spend, so it's not unreasonable to expect the same behavior

157

of our customers. In addition, we know that as salespeople we would never say "no" on behalf of our customers, so we want to give customers every opportunity to speak for themselves.

In answer to the salesperson's question, "How much did you want to spend today," the customer tells you, "About $500 less." If you can, find an alternative item that's in your customer's price range and show it. The question now is, do you give Feature-Advantage-Benefits to the lower-priced item or not? The answer lies in deciding which item you would really like to sell at this point. Well, unless you're a wimpering, simpering sack of jello, you still want to sell the more expensive one. I know I do! Don't give up hope. Remember, all shoppers at one time or another have spent more than they planned on, or more than their budget allowed. How you choose to demonstrate the alternative can make or break your chance of maximizing the sale.

Keep the more expensive item with you when you show the customer the lesser-priced article, if you can. Without doing anything to embellish the lower-priced article, just ask the customer: "How about this one?" It's likely that your customer will see the lower-priced item as a poor second to the first item. After all, you have created excitement and enthusiasm and added a lot of value to the more expensive item. However, you have done nothing to enhance the second article:

Salesperson: What do you think of *this* bicycle? (showing the alternative)

Customer: It's really not as nice. I think I'm losing some speed with that one, aren't I?

Salesperson: Yes, this is more of a touring bike.

Customer: Well, I don't think I like it as well.

Salesperson: I understand. This one (returning to the first bike) is a lot faster. One of the things I forgot to tell you about this one is . . .

You have made a smart move in not saying anything to enhance the lower-priced article, because you have just given yourself another opportunity to add value to, and close the sale on, the higher-priced item.

If by chance, the customer likes the less expensive item, go ahead and give an FABG on it. Certainly you want to make the sale, whether it's for the higher-priced item or the lower-priced one. Watch the customer for clues before you decide which route to take.

If the customer shows any hesitation either verbally or physically, go for making the sale on the more expensive item. Responses like, "I don't like this one as well," or "It's okay," or "This one's not *bad*," indicate a lack of enthusiasm by the customer to consider the alternative. Even the way they touch, hold, or look at the item can be a signal. Think of how you react when you open presents on your birthday. If you love something, you're expressions and actions are completely different from those when you're forced to act politely excited over a gift you could definitely live without.

On the other hand, customers may show interest in the alternative by immediately picking it up or touching it without hesitation or prompting by the salesperson. Or they may say, "Oh, *this* one's not bad." Even the emphasis on a particular word in their response may give you a clue as to how to proceed.

If customers' final objection is their inability to afford either the expensive item or the less costly article, and you are reasonably certain that budget is the problem, this is the time to talk about alternate ways to pay:

Customer: The more expensive strand is beautiful, but it's still just so much money.

Salesperson: Well, I have an idea. We have a financing plan here that will make it pretty easy on you with monthly payments, and you can take the piece home with you now. Would you like to get started on the paperwork? I just know you're going to be happy with this one.

Use financing plans, layaway plans, anything that will make it easier on the customer, as the last resort in overcoming objections. These are terrific closes when the customer wants the item but doesn't have the cash today, or finds it less threatening to look at the higher price in terms of monthly payments rather than the total price.

Closing the sale by offering to hold the merchandise for the customer should also be only a last resort. Apparel salespeople are the most famous for using this strategy too early in the objection-handling process, like right out of the gate. The lack of success of doing so can be proven by tracking the number of articles put on hold that never get picked up.

In fact, with one chain of over 200 women's apparel stores, I asked managers to estimate the dollar amount of articles on hold in their back rooms on any particular day. They came up with a range of between $500 to as much as $3,500 per store. When added up, it came to a whopping $360,000 worth of merchandise on hold across the chain. And naturally, out of that $360,000, over 95 percent of the merchandise on hold was hot new merchandise that was even more likely to sell if it had been on the floor for an extra day or two days. Instead, it was being hidden in the hold section of the back room, waiting for customers never again to return.

The salespeople don't even have to be the ones to suggest holding merchandise. Customers have figured out that by asking for an item to be put on hold, they are free to leave. So "Can you hold this for me," can be a stall, just like "I want to shop around."

The Eleventh Commandment

All of us occasionally make the mistake of judging others by outward appearances. Sometimes we decide that the way people dress or the kind of job they have determines what their price range is. This is just another form of negatively qualifying our customers, instead of giving them the opportunity to make decisions for themselves.

Avoid deciding for the customer. Furthermore, remember the Eleventh Commandment (in the Salesperson's Bible). Keep it and its corollaries as a sacred trust:

*IT IS EASIER TO COMETH DOWN IN PRICE
THAN IT IS TO PUSHETH UP*

**Thou Shalt Never Decide for the Customer What the
Customer Wisheth to Spend; and**

**Thou Shalt Show Some Spirit and Starteth by
Demonstrating Superior Quality Merchandise**

The flow chart provided will help you see the process of handling objections in its entirety. Use it as you would a road map. Study it thoroughly so you can use it when your customers voice objections. When you do, you will find that "Mr. and Mrs. Be-Back" can easily become "Mr. and Mrs. Buy Now."

A ROAD MAP
TO HANDLING CUSTOMER OBJECTIONS

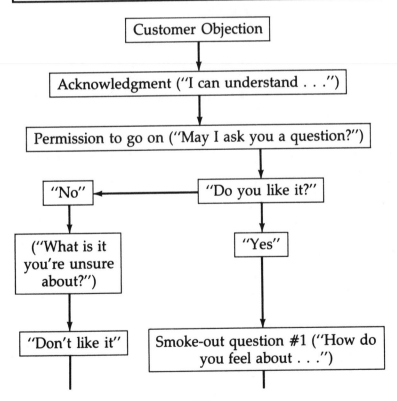

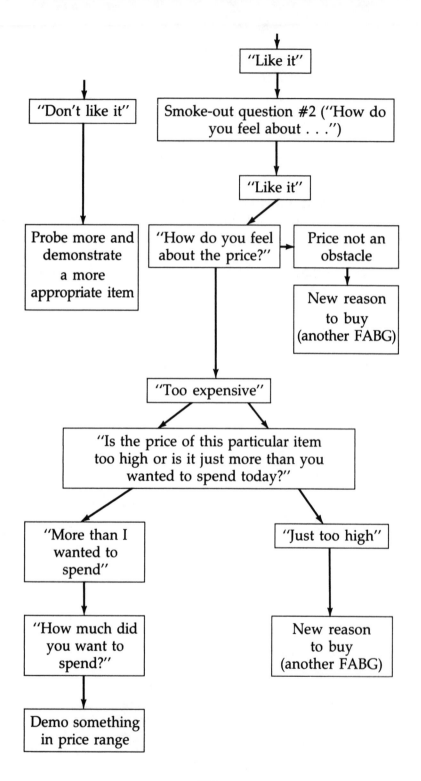

HOT TIPS AND KEY INSIGHTS

- Handling objections is an essential part of the sales process because you can't get to the close if there are obstacles in the way. You need to be able to identify the customer's objections if you want to overcome them.

- Usually when customers object, they are giving you an incomplete or false reason for not buying. Sometimes they do not know what they want. Mostly, it's because they don't trust you or find value in the merchandise.

- To uncover the customer's real objections, you have to be empathetic, put yourself "on the customer's side," and take a caring approach to what is happening in the customer's mind.

- Verbatim, use the six-step technique to smoke out the real objection: Listen to the customer's entire objection without interruption; acknowledge the objection by repeating it word for word, preceded by the words, "I can understand," or "I can appreciate"; and seek permission to ask a question by saying, "May I ask a question," to which the answer will invariably be, "Yes." Then:

- Ask broad-based questions, the first one of which is always, "Do you like the item," followed by as many other questions as you need to uncover the true objection.

- Smoke out the true objection by a series of specific questions based on the FABGs you used during the demonstration to make sure that the benefits you emphasized were the benefits that were important to the customer.

- Ask the customer about price, always as a last resort, and always phrased as the non-threatening, "How do you feel about the price?"

- To overcome additional objections, present other benefits of the merchandise. This can only be done if you saved some ammunition for later use.

- If the price is the real inhibiting factor, determine whether the customer thinks the merchandise is not worth the cost, or costs more than the customer wanted to spend.

- If the objection is about value, add more value to the merchandise by providing more FABGs. If the objection is about budget, ask the dreaded question: "How much did you want to spend today?" When the customer tells you, show merchandise in the customer's price range without enhancing it. The customer may return to the original merchandise because it is clearly of better quality.

- If the customer wants the merchandise and price is still a factor, you can suggest whatever layaway, installment or other credit plans your store has to offer.

CHAPTER SEVEN

CLOSING THE SALE

**The desire a salesperson has to make a sale
is more important than the technique he or she uses.**

I was on a client's selling floor one evening (after doing a sales training seminar during the day) and I had been working with a married couple for over an hour. Again, I had all of the salespeople watching me and I was sweating bullets on this one. I must have handled four different objections, talked about financing, layaway, etc. I pulled out all the stops, used every closing technique I could think of that was appropriate, and this couple would not crack.

The situation called for a drastic measure. I went into the back room and picked up one of the workbooks from the seminar that day. I put it on the counter in front of the couple and started going through it. "Look, I just went to this sales course today and I've done everything it says to do in here. You should have bought by now. What's the problem?" They laughed, and they bought!

Why does closing the sale evoke such emotion in the hearts and minds of salespeople? I just know someone out there has opened the book to this chapter and these are the very first words they will read.

If you have been reading from the beginning of this book you know that closing is at the same time the least and most important step in the selling process. It is the least important because the customer should have said "I'll take it" and there would be no need to read on. And it becomes the most important step because if they don't say "I'll take it," you will *have* to ask them to buy.

This is business. And a very serious business at that. Many people count on your ability to turn shoppers into buyers. A store's success is dependent upon the number of individuals who reach their selling goals.

INTENT IS EVERYTHING

It is nearly impossible to help anyone who does not have the ambition or the intent to be successful. It's difficult to make excuses for them and I find it beyond my scope to give them techniques that will help them want to succeed. Tough talk I know. It is a lot more fun to work with people who want to win and merely want the techniques and strategies to get there.

I have always said that I would rather calm salespeople down than have to light a fire under their fannies. Pushiness and aggressiveness is nothing more than a lack of technique. People who have to be prodded to close the sale may find a happier life outside of selling.

Do you love people? Do you go nuts when you close a big one? Do you have lows that seem very low, when you're not making lots of sales? Is it one of your favorite things in life when a customer says YES? If you said yes to all of these questions, then welcome to the subject of closing the sale, the final commitment.

Every customer has a different set of values and expectations. Each also brings different experiences and knowledge of the products and services you offer. So to give you a formula for closing the sale that would routinely work with every customer would be impossible.

Maybe it's more important at this point to again remind you that doing it, actually attempting to close the sale, is more important than any specific technique you might use. The attempt to close and the corresponding reflection on what you did right and wrong serve as the best teacher in learning to close the sale.

In the United States today, out of 100 sales presentations made by retail salespeople, the following statistics continue to hold true:

- Twenty percent of the time customers say, "I'll take it" on their own.
- Twenty percent of the time the salesperson asks for the sale.
- Sixty percent of the time no attempt is made to close.

I have chosen not to give you one hundred examples of salespeople who didn't close who could have. Why? You know exactly where you stand on this subject. Just look at your close rate to see if you need to get better.

GETTING STARTED

Before we go any further let's clearly define where we are in the presentation. You have closed the sale once by using a trial close. At this point the customer has given you an objection to the primary item you demonstrated. Or during your demonstration the customer voiced an objection to what you showed. As you went through the process, you handled the customer's concerns, which should now prompt you to take positive action and gain commitment:

Salesperson: How about a high-impact, plastic carrying case to protect your son's new saxophone?

Customer: I'm really not sure. It's a great instrument but I know I should think about spending that much money for a musical instrument I'm not even sure Johnny will continue to play.

Salesperson: I can certainly appreciate you wanting to think about it. You want to make sure Johnny is going to make a commitment to his music don't you?

Customer: I sure do!

Salesperson: May I ask you a question?

Customer: Sure.

Salesperson: Do you think Johnny will like the saxophone?

Customer: Of course. He really wants one.

Salesperson: Well, that's a start. How do you feel about this particular model for him?

Customer: I'm a little concerned that it may be too big.

Salesperson: I know what you mean about the size. Fortunately, the sax won't continue to grow over the next few months and years but as you know, Johnny will. And it won't be long before it seems like just the right size. You know, I forgot to tell you something. This saxophone is special for a couple of reasons. One, it is very easy for a beginner to play, which will make it a lot of fun to practice rather than the drag it seems to be for some kids to make a decent sound. And I'm sure you won't mind hearing music you can recognize, will you?

Customer: It sure will help!

Now what? This is it: the moment of truth. It's time to close the sale. What do you say to close the sale and make sure that Mom is happy to make the purchase? Again, there is no guaranteed formula for closing a sale, as evidenced by the hundreds of closing techniques used every day by thousands of salespeople worldwide. Some closing techniques have been around for 50 years or more. Some work better than others. Some are easier to remember than others.

Although your first impulse might be to learn as many closing techniques as possible, you probably won't succeed if that's all you do. Chances are you'll forget the techniques when you need them, or you'll get two or three techniques confused and possibly misfire. I favor closing techniques that can be remembered and easily used.

BASIC CLOSING TECHNIQUES

Start with a few basic closes and practice only those first. Be as creative as you can and try not to revert back to the tired closing lines we've all heard before. For example, telling your customers that your store may be going out of business or that you desperately need the sale to put your kids through college are not the most professional ways of closing the sale and won't serve you well, either. They're actually kind of pathetic closing lines if you look at it from the customer's perspective.

Here are some tried and true professional approaches that can work well for you in most selling situations:

The Either/Or Close

Either/or questions discourage the customer from saying no to your request for the sale. Instead of saying, "Would you like to buy something?" (to which any customer can readily answer yes or no), ask the customers if they would like to buy "X" or if they would like to buy "Y." Or would they like to pay with "X" or pay with "Y"?

All it takes are questions like, "Would you like to pay with cash or charge?" or "Would you like to pay by check or cash?" (Checks cost your store less than credit cards do!) By giving your customer several ways in which to tell you they want the merchandise, you've enhanced your opportunity to get a yes answer and close the sale. This is especially appropriate for those customers who are ready to buy, but just need to be prompted.

Customer: I think I like this dress better than the other one.

Salesperson: I agree with you. It's flattering on you. By the way, should I gift wrap it to make it more special for you, or should I put it in a box?

Customer: Wrap it. That sounds like fun.

By agreeing to have it wrapped, the customer is saying yes to the closing question. She may have also said yes if asked, "Would you like to take this dress," but she would have had a bigger opportunity to say no.

The Reflexive Close

I like this method because it is straightforward and works. Suppose you're working with a couple who love a particular bedroom set. You have successfully demonstrated the value of this bedroom set and now you feel that they are waiting to be asked to buy.

If one of them says, "Can the furniture be delivered by Wednesday?" most salespeople say, "Yes." Even if you know it can be delivered by Wednesday, *don't say it.* Instead, immediately respond with a closing question such as, "Would you like delivery on Wednesday?" or "What time could we deliver on Wednesday?"

If he or she says "Yes" to your closing question, you've made the sale. Of course, keep your promise.

This is called the reflexive technique because it turns the question *back* to the customer. Here are some other examples of this reflexive closing technique that also indicate successful attempts to add on to the original sale:

Customer: Could I get this bike in a navy blue color?
Salesperson: Would you like it in navy?
Customer: Yes, I really would.
Salesperson: Okay, great. How about a durable rack to make carrying your books easy?
OR
Customer: Does this perfume come in a larger bottle?
Salesperson: Would you like a larger bottle?
Customer: Yes, it might last longer.
Salesperson: Well, you're in luck because I've got the largest size they make right here. Would you like some powder to go with that?

As indicated above, capitalize on your opportunities to add on. If you don't, your closing techniques are only half-baked. By purchasing anything, your customers have already demonstrated that they like your store and trust your judgement. Why not capitalize on it?

170

A caution: When using the Reflexive Close, be careful to avoid using, "If I could, would you . . ." language. Suppose a customer said, "I wish I could find a laser printer for my computer that's under $1,000," and you responded with, "If I could find you a laser printer for under $1,000, would you buy it today?" You would be guilty of the "If I could, would you . . ." technique.

This is an outdated closing technique and will only gain you disrespect from your customers. Get into the 90s; customers are sophisticated enough to see through slick sales techniques.

The Ask-For-It Close

This technique usually requires more courage than some of the other closing techniques and, as a result, is often avoided by many salespeople. Yet, the Ask-For-It Close can often provide the most effective means of pushing an indecisive customer over the fence.

When customers can't decide on a purchase, sometimes you've got to relax, smile, laugh a bit and ask them to buy. Start with a bold question that asks the customer, "So, would you like to buy it?" Do this with a bit of humor even if you're not a funny person most of the time. Most customers will appreciate your candor and enjoyment of the situation. Here is some supporting language:

Customer: I'm sorry to take up so much of your time, but I can't make up my mind.

Salesperson: No problem; I'll make it up for you. Shall I gift wrap it?

OR

Customer: It's late. Maybe I'll come in tomorrow to buy it.

Salesperson: Oh, please. Don't you think you have suffered long enough? Why don't you buy it now for my sake?

OR

Customer: I like this so much, but I know I don't need it and my husband will die when he sees the price.

Salesperson:	Look, I know you want it. Why don't you put yourself out of your misery and buy it? I think you owe it to yourself.

Remember, have some fun with this one. Your enthusiasm and enjoyment on the sales floor will be readily apparent to your customers and will most likely be transmitted to everyone in the store. Having fun on the sales floor, after all, is the spirit of what retail selling is all about.

Add-On Close

This is an outstanding closing technique because it endeavors to both sell an item and add on to it at the same time. Basically, it's like asking, "What do you think about this with that?" This close also gives you some place to go once you've solved an objection.

Customer:	Are these CD prices for real? Cassette tapes never used to cost this much!
Salesperson:	I'm afraid our prices are as low as you'll find anywhere in town. It's amazing, isn't it? How about a CD case to carry your new CDs in?

OR

Customer:	I've never worn yellow because it's never been flattering to my skin.
Salesperson:	I know the feeling, but this yellow looks great on you. How about a scarf to jazz up your outfit a bit?

Add-on closes can go on forever. That's the beauty of add-ons—either you make the sale or you keep trying until the customer finally says "no." Think of it as a giant window of opportunity to close the sale.

Third-Party Reference Close

Since most customers are not total innovators when it comes to buying new merchandise, sometimes you've got to give your customer another reason to buy even after establishing sufficient value for the product. The third-party reference close is intended to add customer confidence when it may still be lacking.

Try this: Let your customer know that someone else you know bought it and is very satisfied with the purchase. This "someone" could be anyone. It could be a customer who recently stopped in to tell you she loved the new perfume you sold her. It could be a friend of yours who purchased a similar item and has been delighted with it. It could even be a sales colleague or the store manager who bought the same piece of merchandise.

Realistically, do you feel more comfortable about purchasing something because the salesperson told you he had recently bought one, too? Yes, we all do. Knowing (or simply believing) someone else has tested the waters and has been satisfied gives customers more confidence to do the same.

Customer:	I've seen these skirts in magazines, but I've never seen anyone wearing one.
Salesperson:	I know what you mean. I live in constant fear of making a bad fashion statement! I do know, however, of several regular customers who have purchased these skirts. They say they're comfortable and go with everything.
Customer:	So you think they're going to be popular this year?
Salesperson:	I certainly do. Why don't you give it a try?
Customer:	Okay. I need to be daring once in a while.
Salesperson:	I thought you'd decide that. How about a coordinating blouse to go with your new skirt?

Or

Customer:	I can't decide between the champagne glasses or the wine glasses.
Salesperson:	It's a tough decision, although my manager told me she usually buys wine glasses as wedding gifts because they're used more often and are less expensive to replace.

Customer:	That's probably true.
Salesperson:	So may I wrap up a set of wine glasses for you today?
Customer:	Sure, let's go for the wine glasses.

The Assumptive Close

If a customer displays little or no sign of resistance during your presentation, try the Assumptive Close. With this technique, you're literally assuming the customer will purchase the item in question. Take the item up to the cash register and hope your customer is following you!

Sure, it's a bold maneuver, but it helps you to tell your customer that you're done talking and the sale is over. How you handle this closing technique, however, is up to you. Some handle it quite aggressively. Others are more subtle, asking something such as, "Well, which one would you like?"

Study the following exchanges to determine which style suits you best:

Customer:	He needs a coat for his birthday. I like this one.
Salesperson:	Great. I'll take this up to the register for you while you look around for some more birthday gifts for your husband.
Customer:	Okay. Thank you.
	OR
Customer:	These VCRs are nice. We've always wanted one in our living room.
Salesperson:	Wonderful. Do you know which one you'd like?
Customer:	I guess we like the one with the remote control feature more than the other one.
Salesperson:	I think that's the best buy you can make on a VCR. I'll tell the cashier to get one out of the stockroom for you.
Customer:	Great. Thanks.

Assumptive closes are useful when your store is busy and you're in a hurry to help as many people as possible Before you try this closing technique though, make sure the customer hasn't demonstrated any resistance to what you're selling. You could find yourself taking several steps backward!

The Order Form Close

Have you ever seen a salesperson who starts writing down information on an order form before the customer even gets close to the register? This is another closing move known as the Order Form Close.

It works this way: Suppose your customers are talking about some changes they would like to make to a particular piece of merchandise. They may want a ring to be sized down or to add an internal hard drive to the computer. With the Order Form Close, your job is to start writing down whatever they want on an actual order form.

Another way of initiating this close is to pull out an order form and start asking for personal information about the customer, like a name and address. If the customer gives you this information without any resistance, you've made the sale. If the customer is not sure about the sale, he or she will let you know. All you have to do in that case is apologize and say you thought that he or she had already decided upon the purchase.

Here's an example of when to use this technique:

Customer: You know, these custom blinds seem to be popular these days. My daughter has them in her dorm room and my neighbor says she's ordered some for her nursery room. Do you have children?

Salesperson: Not yet. Would you please spell your last name for me?

Customer: Sure. It's Finster. That's F-I-N-S-T-E-R.

Salesperson: And your first name?

The salesperson here capitalizes on having a talkative customer to make the sale. You can also try this on custom-

175

ers who can't seem to make up their minds, but be careful to use the order form technique only with appropriate customers. Someone who is naturally suspicious of sales-people might take great offense at your assumptions.

The "To The Bone" Close

Everyone in sales has haggled with a customer over price at one time or another. Few salespeople know how to use this situation to their advantage. Using the "To The Bone" Close can appease your price-driven customer by making that person feel like you're trying to get the lowest price, even though you know you probably can't. Here's an example:

Customer: I would love it if this armoire was only $100 less.

Salesperson: Would you like this armoire for $100 less?

Customer: Yes, I would.

Salesperson: Well, let me try and see what I can do. I'll be right back. (Salesperson disappears into the back; customer awaits response.)

Salesperson: Gee, I'm sorry but I couldn't get the man-ager to approve a price reduction. It seems there's no margin left to play with since the price of the armoire is already so low. It is a tremendous value already.

Customer: I see.

Salesperson: You know you really like it. Shall I start the paperwork?

Customer: Sure. I've been saving space in my bedroom for one of these for months.

The "To the Bone" close helps you get around the sticky issue of price. Although in the preceding example, the salesperson never got the discount the customer wanted, he eventually made the final sale because a genuine willing-ness to help the customer was demonstrated.

By showing that you want to get the best deal for the customer, you can get your customer more emotionally involved in the sale. In the example, while the salesperson was checking on the possibility of a price reduction for the armoire, the customer was probably thinking, "Oh, I hope I get it, I hope I get it." She cared about getting the price reduction, but by allowing her hopes to be raised, she also grew to care more about having the armoire itself.

The more emotional the customer gets about a piece of merchandise, the easier it will be to sell that merchandise.

Conversely, if the same salesperson had immediately said, "No, we don't discount here," it would have completely cut off communication with the customer who, having become discouraged, would probably have left without another look.

If your store doesn't have a back room in which you can pretend to be consulting with your manager, ask your manager to pretend he is talking with you about the customer's request for a discount. When you're using the "To the Bone" Close you have to give an effective performance.

The "Do Something Different" Close

When all else fails, don't hesitate to do something totally off the wall to get our customer's attention fixed upon the final sale. Again, use a little humor here. If you're having fun on the sales floor, your customers will generally have fun, too.

One suggestion for a "Do Something Different" Close is to ask the customer if he or she wants you to call the person for whom the item is being bought.

Customer:	There are so many choices. How do your customers ever make up their minds?
Salesperson:	Well, in cases like yours, we usually call up the person you're buying for (said jokingly) and ask them if they'd like it. Shall we try this?
Customer:	I suppose we might have to if I don't make up my mind! (Said laughingly!)

177

Customers may drive you crazy but if they haven't walked out the door, you still have a shot at closing the sale. It may take something completely imaginative, but it's worth a try. It's your job, remember?

I once took a lady's purse, turned it upside down, found a quarter in the contents that dropped out and said, "What do you mean you don't have enough for a layaway deposit?" I know what you're thinking—"Harry, you've gone too far this time!" But you have to know that I would never have done such a thing if I hadn't established a great rapport with the customer and knew I could get away with it. It worked. She was nearly hysterical laughing, and so were several other customers, too. Warning: I don't advocate using this technique more than once in a lifetime!

The Penalty Close

Cross this closing technique off your list. Like "slick salesman" techniques, it's too overused in today's retail selling environment to be effective.

Penalty closing statements come in the form of, "Our only sale of the year ends tomorrow," "This is positively the last one we have in stock," or "It probably won't be here tomorrow." Penalty closing ends up penalizing your customers for wanting to spend money in your store:

I'm afraid this is the last one, so you'd be wise to buy it now.

The sale is over tomorrow and I'm sure you won't find a discount like this any time soon.

These kinds of statements are unpleasant for customers and may only convince them to visit another store where there are no penalties for wanting to spend money.

If for some reason you decide you have to tell the customer something that resembles a penalty statement, don't make it sound like such a penalty. Try this approach instead:

Salesperson: This is the last one I have in stock. I certainly don't expect it to sell before tomorrow night, but I wanted to let you know.

Customer:	Oh, thank you. I appreciate your telling me. Maybe I *ought to go ahead* and buy it now.
Salesperson:	It might be a good idea.
	OR
Salesperson:	If you don't have time to purchase it now, why don't you put it on hold? That way no one else can buy it tomorrow.
Customer:	That sounds good; let's do it.
Salesperson:	Great. May I get your name and phone number and the time you'll be returning to purchase it tomorrow?
Customer:	Sure.

HANDLING REQUESTS FOR DISCOUNTS

The competitive nature of the retail selling environment today is such that many retailers have had to resort to a variety of techniques to maintain their volume. It is also the case that many customers want to haggle with you over the price of a piece of merchandise. A customer's request for a discount, even if approved by management, may not always be the setting for an easy close.

Suppose you encounter a customer who appears genuinely interested in a particular item, but who is also asking for a discount. If you perceive the discount to be absolutely necessary and are able to convince your manager of this fact, you may get some or all of the discount authorized. Politely excuse yourself (as you witnessed earlier with the "To The Bone" closing technique) and consult with your manager about lowering the price.

Let's say that your manager gives approval for a partial discount. Be careful to let the customer know that you don't make this a regular habit and you are only doing it because you know he really wants the item and you want to see that he gets it. Also, at all times, keep information concerning discounts like you would valuables—in a safe—as you don't want your store to earn a reputation as an easy discounter.

If the customer is still unhappy with the partial discount offered, then ask the customer for a commitment. That is, ask how he will be paying for the item and whether you can show proof of this to your manager for a second try at a discount. If the customer is willing to do this, you can pretty much assume the deal can be done with a discount.

Once the manager authorizes any necessary discount, return to the customer and congratulate him. Let your customer know that a discount of this size is a big deal in your store and that it was a direct result of your tireless efforts. By doing this, you will condition your customers to feel like they've "made out," rather than giving them the impression that they can come into your store and negotiate anytime they want to.

If the manager doesn't grant you the discount, blame it on the cost of the merchandise rather than on people. You can't afford to harm your customer relationships.

Customer:	I think your store has the best selection of leather briefcases, but these prices are too high. Is $450 the best you can give me on this one?
Salesperson:	I understand your concern. However, we don't offer discounts because we don't initially inflate our prices. That's how we're able to offer the best value in leather goods to our customers.
Customer:	Well, I can appreciate that, but I'm not in any position to spend more than $350.
Salesperson:	Of course. Well, since I can tell you really like this particular briefcase, I'd certainly be willing to ask my manager about a discount for you. I would like to see you get it. Do you mind waiting? (Disappears to find the manager.)
Salesperson:	Well, I couldn't get authorization for a $100 discount, but I did get authorization for a $50 discount which is still a substantial savings. Shall I write it up for you?
Customer:	No, I'm sorry. I just can't spend more than $350 on a briefcase. I guess I'll have to look around a little more.

Salesperson: Wait. I know you want this briefcase and I want you to have it. May I ask what type of payment you were planning to use? If I can show my manger that you're committed to buying this briefcase, maybe he would reconsider the $100 discount. It can't hurt to try.

Customer: That's a good idea. Let's see. I think I've got $100 in cash and the rest could be paid with a personal check.

Salesperson: (Takes the money and goes to consult with the manager again.) Well, we're in luck. The manager checked the our cost and found some extra margin, so I can sell you the briefcase for $350. Let me tell you that the cash really helped. Otherwise, I don't think we could have done it. Do you want me to wrap it up?

Customer: No, I'm going to use it immediately.

Salesperson: Congratulations. I'm really glad this worked out.

Notice in this scenario how the salesperson:

1) Talked about how the store did not inflate prices;
2) Stressed that the merchandise was already a good value;
3) Said that discounts rarely occurred in the store.

If you have determined that there is nothing you can do to make a price-driven customer happy, my advice is to tell these "retail deal-makers," in a direct yet polite manner, that your store does not offer discounts because your prices are reasonable to begin with.

This approach will either dissuade the impossible-to-please customer, or it will encourage him to further analyze the value of the merchandise in question.

TURNING OVER THE SALE

Turning over the sale, or T.O.s as they are commonly called, can be an important component of closing the sale.

The T.O. is another sales technique that helps you maximize your opportunity with each customer who walks through the door. T.O.s offer you a solution in situations when you are personally unable to close the sale.

Even if you are the most terrific salesperson in the world, you simply can't sell everybody. There are problems inherent in every sales situation—sometimes you can overcome these problems—other times you cannot.

By employing another salesperson who stands a better chance of closing the sale, you enable both the customer and the store to win. The customer wins because his needs have been met; the store wins because its investment is realized. You also win as a salesperson because you made half of an additional sale (commissions on T.O.s are usually split evenly) that might not have occurred without the T.O.

When To T.O. The Sale

The most common problems that occur in sales situations are caused by some type of personality or image conflict (as we saw in Chapter 2), a lack of technical expertise or the basic inability to close.

Personality Conflicts

We can all understand the problem of personal conflicts. No one can expect to be liked by everyone. If a customer doesn't like you, don't take it personally or as a reflection upon your sales ability. You might have elephant-breath and got too close. Or, it could be because of something completely absurd like the color of your hair, the width of your tie or the glasses you wear. Some customers have bizarre hang-ups that you can't even begin to deal with. Personality or image conflicts happen all of the time to some of the best salespeople in the world.

Take the man who is shopping with his wife. If you're an attractive female salesperson, that customer's wife may not be interested in having her husband spend time with you as you try to close the sale. You may remind other customers of their mother or father, whom they resent. And, no matter what you say or do, they're going to think about that person they hate much more than what they came in to buy. Therefore, your best bet is to turn over the sale to someone who doesn't remind the customer of a dreaded parent.

Here are some other situations that may require a T.O.:

- Customer doesn't like the way you dress; maybe you're too trendy or too conservative and the customer doesn't feel you could make a fair decision.
- Customer feels you're too young or too old, thinking, "That person can't possibly know what he's talking about."
- Customer doesn't like your gender. Male customers, for example, often get uncomfortable when women are helping them select clothes.
- Customer doesn't understand your language or the way you speak. Foreign or physically impaired customers often need special treatment.
- The customer is prejudiced. Unfortunately, this is true all over the world. If you detect it, T.O.—ASAP.

Lack of Knowledge

Another common problem many salespeople experience is a lack of knowledge or technical expertise about a particular piece of merchandise. Too many salespeople, whether through ignorance or selfishness, feel they have to answer every customer's question themselves. Actually, the converse is true.

If you don't know the answer to a customer's question, seek help from someone who does know the answer. Trying to fake knowledge, especially technical expertise with a customer, is like kissing a sale goodbye. You've lost your credibility, and the customer is sure to know it:

Customer:	So, can I use these batteries with my Sony Walkman?
Salesperson:	Yeah, I think so. I don't know why you couldn't.
Customer:	Are you sure? I hate having to return things.

Salesperson: Yeah, I'm pretty sure.

Does this salesperson sound convincing to you? Probably not. Think how easy it could have been for that salesperson to have asked the manager if those batteries did indeed work with the customer's Sony Walkman, or for that salesperson to have invited another salesperson over to talk with the customer about the particular size of batteries suitable for a Sony Walkman. By doing so, the salesperson could have found the right answer for the customer and most likely have closed the sale or facilitated the closing of the sale with little trouble.

Inability to Close

The most common problem that occurs in sales situations is when you are just plain unable to close the sale. This can result from a lack of practice on your part, but it can also result from an unwillingness on the part of the customer to let you close the sale. If the customer is not giving you very good indicators that include nodding of the head, listening intently, asking questions, etc., something is not clicking.

In these instances, you owe it to the store and the customer to T.O. the sale. Give the customer a chance to talk to someone else in the store who might be able to serve him or her better. Before you T.O. the sale however, make sure that the customer still has a range of purchasing options. You don't want to limit what your colleague might be able to do.

How to T.O. The Sale

Obviously, T.O.s involve a teamwork approach to selling, which requires practice. Also, every salesperson in the store needs to have the interests and needs of the customer at heart rather than his or her own.

The most important element when you're getting ready to T.O. a sale is to hand the customer over to an expert. Don't wait for the customer's permission—just do it.

Here are some specific guidelines for turning over a sale:

1. EXPLAIN to your customer that you are bringing someone else into the conversation who might be able to
   better answer questions about the merchandise:

*You know, Mr. Jones, you're talking about the limited edition prints
and I've got someone here who's an expert on this year's limited
edition prints. He may be able to help you best, since I know you're
really interested in this type of art piece. Steve, will you step over
here for a minute, please?*

OR

*Mrs. Green, I don't feel I'm doing a good job of explaining this
merchandise to you. Let me find someone else who is more familiar
with the taste of teenagers so your needs will be met. Sarah, will
you step over here for a minute, please?*

2. Politely INTRODUCE your customer to the new salesperson and review the details of the situation:

Salesperson #1: Steve, this is Mr. Jones.

Salesperson #2: How do you do, Mr. Jones?

Customer: Fine, thank you.

Salesperson #1: Mr. Jones is interested in the limited edition prints. Since you're the on-site ex-
pert, I thought you would be better
equipped to answer Mr. Jones' questions.

Salesperson #2: My pleasure.
OR

Salesperson #1: Sarah, this is Mrs. Smith.

Salesperson #2: How do you do, Mrs. Smith?

Customer: Fine, thank you very much.

Salesperson #1: Sarah, I've been showing Mrs. Smith
some charm bracelets and she's not sure
which one will be appropriate for her
daughter. I thought since you're the expert, you might be able to help.

Salesperson #2: Absolutely.

3. MOVE AWAY from the sale once you have made the turnover:

Mr. Jones, it was my pleasure to help you. I'll be leaving you in good hands now and will check back in a moment to make sure you're getting all your questions answered.

> OR

Mrs. Smith, I was delighted to work with you and will certainly check back to make sure you're finding out what you need to know.

Whenever you turn over sales, it is important that you make the customers feel that a T.O. will help them make the right selection of merchandise. In this way, rather than feeling manipulated, your customers will feel reinforced.

BUYING SIGNALS

I have talked at length about closing the sale right after handling an objection. There are, however, many times during the presentation, when it is not only appropriate to close but necessary. It is the result of hearing a "buying signal."

Buying signals are just that—signals that the customer is ready and willing to buy. Buying signals are not always easy or obvious to spot. Your antenna has to really be out to recognize them. They can be very subtle and difficult to hear, and sometimes they are physical. The customer's body language and actions sometimes speak louder than words.

The biggest danger in not recognizing a buying signal is that with additional dialogue from the salesperson after a buying signal, you may accidentally buy the merchandise back:

Customer: These boots are the best I have ever seen.

Salesperson: They also have an odor-absorbing liner inside.

Customer: Oh. I had something once in a shoe like that and I didn't like it at all. Never mind.

To understand buying signals, first note that they generally come after value has been established. Without value the customer may be just asking you questions. After value, customers are clarifying and if your answer is acceptable, they may buy.

Customer: What other colors are available?
(This is a question. The customer needs more information.)

Customer: Can I get it in black?
(This is a buying signal.)

Just remember: when the customer gives a buying signal, it is time to close the sale.

One of my favorite examples of a buying signal missed is in this dialogue:

Salesperson: What brings you into our store today?

Customer: My cousin Bernie was in last week and purchased the most beautiful chair I've ever seen.

The vast majority of salespeople continue the probing process to see what kind of chair or even what cousin Bernie looks like. It is a missed buying signal. "Bernie" is trust and "the most beautiful I have ever seen" is value. Close the sale.

Salesperson: What brings you into our store today?

Customer: My cousin Bernie was in last week and purchased the most beautiful chair I have ever seen!

Salesperson: Would you like one just like it?

At best, this response is a close. At worst, it is a probing question that will get you additional information. Here are examples of 15 buying signals to help you learn what to listen for.

1. Can I get it delivered next week?
2. How long is the guarantee?
3. How long will it take to assemble?
4. That may be one of the most beautiful (blank) I've ever seen.

5. I think it looks great. What do you think?
6. Do they make a slightly smaller model?
7. WOW!
8. How much money do I have to put down?
9. How many do you think I need?
10. Have you sold many of these before?
11. Can you throw in the shipping?
12. Do you gift wrap?
13. What is your return policy?
14. What kind of credit cards do you take?
15. Is it sturdy enough? You know I have three kids.

Closing can be fun.

Believe it or not, closing should become fun for you. After you become a confident closer I'm sure you will have a larger appetite for the hundreds of closing techniques that are out there. At this point you may want to take a trip down to the store to pick up more books to further your study.

No matter what you read and study, remember that your close should be a logical finishing step to a great presentation.

HOT TIPS AND KEY INSIGHTS

- There is no magic solution or perfect recipe for getting the customer to buy every time, and for nearly every customer who walks into your store, there is a different closing technique. You can learn enough closing techniques, however, to get your customers to buy almost every single time.

- You must ask for the sale, no matter what. Too many salespeople believe that if they don't feel good about their performance with a customer in the store, then they are no longer obligated to close the sale.

- Ask the customer to buy . . . every single time. Your sole reason for being is *to cause the transfer of merchandise ownership from the store to the customer via a sales slip.* Ask the customer to buy more.

- Buying signals are the essential ingredient to becoming an expert closer. By listening for and acting immediately upon buying signals, you'll soon be able to close sales more often and more quickly than you thought you could.

- A buying signal is when a customer says, "I'll take it," but not in so obvious a manner as that. Buying signals are important because they can help you close the sale at the appropriate moment, rather than waste any additional time.

- Buying signals are typified by statements such as: "Do you have shoes to match this?" "How quickly can you engrave this ring?" "How many of these do you have left?" "Do you accept credit cards?" These statements tell you to stop adding value in the form of another Feature-Advantage-Benefit-Grabber because your customers already believe the merchandise represents value.

- A customer can indicate he or she is ready to buy in hundreds of ways. If you practice listening to your customer's every word, you will quickly develop the skills necessary to pick up on buying signals.

- Some customers never give buying signals. Some buying signals are so vague there's no way to detect them in a conversation. In all cases, you have to take control of the situation yourself: go for the close anyway.

- Learn a few basic closing methods, such as: the Either/Or Close, the Reflexive Close, the Ask-For-It-Close, the Third Party Reference Close, the Assumptive Close, the Order Form Close, and the "To the Bone" Close.

- If customers seek a discount and you see it as crucial to the sale, let customers know that you don't make this a regular habit; you are only doing it because you know they want the item and you want to see that they get it. Keep a tight lid on every discount you make because you do not want your store to earn a reputation as an easy discounter.

- Turning over the sale can be an important component of closing the sale. You can't sell everybody, and by employing another salesperson who stands a better chance of closing the sale, you enable both the customer and the store to win.

- The most important element when turning over a sale is to hand the customer over to an expert. Don't wait for the customer's permission—just do it.

- As you practice closing techniques, remind yourself that it's your responsibility to ask for the sale. Sure, it's easier when the customer says, "I'll take it," but how many times have you heard that? You've got to be prepared to ask for the sale. There are no two ways about it.

CHAPTER EIGHT

CONFIRMATIONS & INVITATIONS

A celebration of thanks . . .

Oh happy day! The money is in the cash register and it's all over. Another satisfied customer. You pat yourself on the back, make a mental note of the commission you just made and get ready to concentrate on the next customer. A few more sales later, the day draws to an end. You feel pretty good. You had a great day in terms of sales, especially because of that one customer that bought what seemed like half of the store. You feel like celebrating so you call your spouse and get a babysitter. It's time for a night out.

The next morning, you wake up feeling as refreshed as you did the night before. You sing in the shower and look forward to going to work. You arrive early, have your second cup of coffee, and take a walk through the store to prepare yourself for yet another great day. It's almost time to open and as one of the other salespeple pushes the button to roll up the gate, you see a pair of shoes waiting to get in. The gate rises to uncover a huge bag (from your

191

store) hanging from the customer's hand. It rises farther and you see a second bag tucked under the customer's arm.

The body looks familiar. Could it be your prized sale from yesterday? No way. She was ecstatic. You could do no wrong with her. The gate seems to be rising in slow motion now. There's her chin, her nose, her eyes . . . oh, no! How can this be? Maybe she got locked in the mall last night and hasn't gone home yet. Fat chance. It looks like you're going to be buying back your great sale.

There are few things worse for salespeople than returns. Never making a sale is one thing, but making it and then losing it is extremely painful. Oh sure, you might be able to save it by making an exchange, but when that doesn't work, it can ruin a perfectly good day.

BUYER'S REMORSE

Buyer's remorse: *bitter regret or guilt over a purchase.* I believe that everyone experiences buyer's remorse to some degree with every single purchase. Food in a restaurant is probably one of the few things you can purchase and not think about returning it afterwards, unless you've just eaten mediocre food in a five-star restaurant. So you can even have buyer's remorse in a restaurant. The minute they put the club sandwich in front of you, you wish you'd ordered the burger.

Buyer's remorse occurs no matter how *much* you spend, too. Think about it. You buy a car, a house, a boat, anything major. You love it. But as soon as you sign on the dotted line, the doubt pops up in your mind. You should've got the other one, you should have waited for interest rates to go down, you should have negotiated a little harder or longer, you should have thought about it a little more, you should have consulted your father, etc., etc., etc.

You buy a new wallet. You pay for it and walk out of the store. The minute you cross the doorway of the store, it begins. You should have looked one more place. Will it take too long for it to bend? Should you have gotten the one with softer leather? Does it look cheap? Will it hold all of your credit cards? You spent too much. Etc., etc., etc.

Buyer's remorse, which most often results in returns or cancellation of purchases, occurs for a variety of reasons.

Do You Like It, Too?

People need approval on everything they do in life, including their purchases. I'm the worst. If people don't notice that I've bought something new, I make a point of showing them—especially with expensive things. I rationalize like crazy to the person I show it to. "It was a lot of money but I think I got a great deal on it, don't you? I mean, I've been working hard. I deserve to treat myself, don't you think? I haven't really bought anything of any consequence for a long time. Really . . . I haven't. Don't you think it's great? I really think so." When I bought that Porsche I talked about in an earlier chapter, I had everyone in the office telling me I did the right thing every time I walked by a desk.

I'm a great customer, though. At least I prompt friends to compliment me. Your worst nightmare is the customer who just hopes someone will pay a compliment. For example, a woman buys a new dress. She wears it to work when? The very next day, of course. You always wear new clothes as soon as possible, right? So in to work she goes in her new dress. Now everyone at work has to know that it's new. They've never seen it before and they see her five days a week. No one compliments her. In fact, no one says anything, not even, "Oh, is that new?" She goes home and hangs it in her closet, never to wear it again and blames the store and you. Or, worse yet, she takes it back to the store.

But if someone at work *does* notice it and pays her a big compliment, she wears it again. If everyone notices and compliments her, she's likely to wear it every other day for the next six months. Your biggest problem as a salesperson in preventing returns is running the risk of no compliments by people who are close to your customer.

People are sometimes so paranoid that even a passing comment can enhance the doubt. A woman in my office bought a ring recently. As I looked at it, I slipped it on my pinkie finger and said, "This would make a nice man's ring." She didn't wear it the next day. She told me she got nervous that she had really bought a man's ring and the salesperson hadn't told her. When she finally did put it back on, three other women in the office were all fussing over it right away. Good-bye buyer's remorse. She hasn't taken it off since.

Knowing that someone else likes what you bought makes you feel confident and happier about your decision. Haven't you experienced this, especially following the purchase of something rather expensive, something you had difficulty deciding upon? Admit it—everyone likes to have their decisions confirmed—even you!

You can't rely, however, upon someone else to tell your customers that they made a wise decision in purchasing whatever you sold them. For one thing, more people live alone today than ever before. You have to take responsibility, otherwise your customers may begin to doubt whether the purchase they made was a wise one. Hence, it is your mission to ask for the sale, and reassure customers about their purchase once the sale is final. After all, *you have the unique opportunity to be the first person to let customers know that they have made the right choice.*

Just Another Human Being

After the transaction is complete and the money is in the register or the order has been signed, you are no longer perceived as a salesperson. You are just another human being in a store. Therefore, complimentary remarks from you will be taken as compliments rather than as typical sales remarks.

*By displaying continued interest in your customer **after** the transaction is made, you can make yourself believable and express sincerity.*

It's a reputation most salespeople never get, but it's one that can have untold advantages. A salesperson who says, "Mrs. Jones, I think you made a wise decision buying this cashmere sweater for your daughter," *after* the sale is rung up, is expressing the fact that she thinks Mrs. Jones really made the right decision. The customer's lingering doubts slowly dissipate.

If you express your approval of a purchase BEFORE the transaction is complete and any money is in the register, you would be saying exactly what the customer expected to hear: more sales talk. If you're saying, "This looks so good on you," or "I'm so glad you decided to buy this one," while still ringing up the purchase at the cash register, you still sound like you're selling, which can be a big turn-off for your customers.

What you're aiming for here is a confirmation of the sale. "Confirmations and Invitations" is a two-part process that helps to eliminate buyer's remorse and the possibility of returns and cancellations, as well as encourage personal trade and repeat business. Let's take a closer look at each part.

THE CONFIRMATION: CEMENTING THE SALE

Confirming your customers' purchases helps to prevent buyer's remorse. As demonstrated above, timing is critical to the effectiveness of your confirmation. But what do you say in a confirmation? That depends upon the specific situation.

Think of this whole process as a "celebration of thanks." Your customer has money. You have merchandise. The customer chose to spend that money in *your* store with *you*. The customer could have spent it anywhere else, but he or she chose not to. You and the customer made a simple exchange of money for merchandise. Neither party owes the other party anything—you're even. But before parting, the salesperson needs to convey the thought, "Hey, thanks for choosing me."

Suppose Mr. and Mrs. Wilson have just purchased a gold locket for their daughter in honor of her graduation from college. She's never worn a locket before and neither Mr. nor Mrs. Wilson is sure their daughter will like one. A confirmation of this particular sale could go like this:

Mr. and Mrs. Wilson, I think you've made an excellent choice for your daughter's graduation present. Not only will its value appreciate over the years, but it will serve to remind your daughter of one of the proudest achievements in life.

Notice in this example how the salesperson not only tells the customers what an excellent choice they made, but also reminds them about one or two benefits that were presumably pointed out in the demonstration. This helps to further cement the sale by reinforcing why the customers purchased the merchandise in the first place. Although every confirmation will be customized for every customer situation, there are guidelines to follow:

1. *Use the customer's name.*
   Having spent the past few minutes with your customer, you probably know his or her name by now. If you don't, look for it on the check, credit card or sales slip. Using individual names like "Mrs. Williams" or "Mr. Peck" is much more personalized than using "Miss" or "Sir."
2. *Use the words "I" and "you."*
   This helps to further personalize the exchange. It's not the store that's thanking the customer; it's you. And you want to be sure to give that customer full credit for making the wise buying decision. You didn't make it.
3. *Confirm why the purchase is a wise one.*
   Tie whatever you say in your confirmation to the reasons for the customer's purchase by reviewing some of the benefits covered during the demonstration. You can also bring up a point the customer mentioned during the probing process. This will alert the customer to the fact that you were indeed listening.

Dialing Away Buyer's Remorse

In the case of very expensive items, like jewelry, furniture, or even an expensive suit, I often recommend a phone-call confirmation. If someone spends $6,000 on a diamond ring in your store, a purchase from which you earn a fairly hefty commission, it's worth an additional two minutes of your time to pick up the phone to let that customer know you think he or she made a great selection.

Whether you call that night (preferable) or the next day, confirmation phone calls are one more effective way of letting customers know they were smart to buy. If merchandise is being special ordered or delivered at a later date, it makes even more sense to call immediately to confirm the sale. That time lag only means there is more time for the customers' friends and family to talk them out of it.

Based upon my experience with customers, I am confident that if you made confirmation phone calls every night to your customers, you would significantly reduce your rate of customer returns and cancellations. Here's an example of a phone confirmation:

Salesperson: Hello, Mr. Trippet?

Customer: Yes.

Salesperson: Mr. Trippet, this is Susan from the China Shop. I was thinking about you after you left the store and had a smile on my face. I feel even more certain that your wife is going to love the pattern you picked out. Every customer of mine admires that pattern and you seemed so happy to purchase it for her. I'm sure she'll love it the minute she sees it.

Customer: I think so, too. Thanks a lot for calling.

While most salespeople are hesitant to do something as bold as calling a customer at home after the sale, most customers genuinely appreciate this gesture. It lets them know that you're thinking about them and their purchase. It serves to eliminate buyer's remorse. And it definitely earns you a better chance of seeing them again . . . for another sale.

THE INVITATION: REQUESTING ANOTHER VISIT

Have you ever had a customer come back and ask specifically for you? Or, how about a customer who was referred to you by a previous customer? Everybody has.

The question is how often? All the time? Sometimes? Occasionally? Never? If the answer is anything but all the time, then this section will be of special interest to you.

Once upon a time, you could gain repeat customers with a simple, "Thanks, and have a nice day." Unfortunately, that's no longer true. Today there are a million other salespeople out there trying to win over YOUR customers.

Obviously, you want to become a better salesperson and earn more money in commissions or bonuses. Consider salespeople who regularly earn in the six-figure salary range. Do you believe this type of salesperson is just lucky? Do they have that much more traffic in their stores than you do? That much traffic *doesn't just walk in every day* and afford salespeople the opportunity to close millions of dollars worth of sales. True, indoor shopping malls may offer large volumes of traffic, but they also foster some of the fiercest competition in retailing. Instead of one women's shoe store, there are five!

In my travels, I have had the great fortune to meet a number of retail salespeople who are truly stand-outs. There are some great ones out there, and when you meet one of them, you know immediately why they are great. I have often talked about Monica Armendariz, who sells women's apparel. At last count, Monica sold $1,200,000 in a year. She's achieved this level of success primarily through building a business of her own within the store. She owns her customers. You know what I mean by *own*? I mean her customers wouldn't think of buying from anyone but her, period. In fact, she told me a great story about a woman getting a $200 gift certificate to Nieman Marcus for her birthday and taking it back for a refund. The customer said, "I can't buy clothes without Monica helping me."

I saw her in action on the floor once and it was fun just watching her. She didn't walk through the store, she ran, and customers ran right after her. She worked a dressing room like a madwoman. But the most impressive thing of all was what she was doing when she didn't have a customer to wait on. I never saw Monica chatting with other salespeople or even taking a short break. She was on the phone calling customers or writing notes to customers during every spare moment for the entire day.

This particular boutique gets a small shipment in nearly every day so the staff has a 15-minute meeting religiously before the store opens every morning. The owner unveils each new garment and gives a basic description of its features and benefits. All of the salespeople are sitting there with their personal trade books, and it resembles an art auction with one exception: the first person to bid gets it. Rumor has it that Monica snags the majority of the new merchandise before it ever hits the floor. She's on the phone like a racehorse out of the starting gate as soon as the meeting is over, calling customers with confidence and determination. "Margie, you've got to come in this afternoon. A dress came in that you have to have. I'm only going to hold it through today." She doesn't ask them to come in, she tells them . . . and they do. Further rumor has it that over 75 percent of everything she holds from the mini-fashion show gets purchased. The owner even has an insurance policy on Monica. Wouldn't you?

Here's one more for you. Four or five years ago I met a man working in a chain of music stores in Minneapolis. His name is Andy Anderson and he's amazing. He has made follow-up a science and is the King of Referrals. He has a book of reference letters from nearly every customer he has ever sold to. And he's got pictures of most of them with their new pianos in their homes, too. In addition, he tracks exactly how each referral came his way so he can send a $25 check to the former customer who is responsible. It's called "bird-dogging." He has practiced "bird-dogging" for some time and has more accurate records than any I've ever seen before. One of his customers received the check in the mail and called him to ask what it was for. He said, "You recommended me to one of your friends about four years ago and he finally bought." Needless to say, the man was amazed.

What's the point? To be really successful in sales, you've got to get your customers to come back to you or send others your way. It's an undisputed fact that it's easier to sell to a repeat or referral customer than to a new one. It's also true that to build a sales practice in any store, you've got to develop customers to become the bread and butter of your existence . . . customers who return time and time again to buy something on each visit, or keep sending you their friends.

I often pose this question to salespeople: Imagine a big black door in your store with your name on it. On the other side of the black door is an exact duplicate of your store. You only get to sell from beyond that black door. And the only way customers can pass through your black door is by asking specifically for you. Could you make a living behind that door? It's an interesting question. If you can, congratulations. You are a sales professional. If you can't, it should be your goal in life.

Tell Your Customers What to Do and They'll Do It!

How many times have you ever heard a salesperson say something like the following?

If you have any questions at all once your washer is installed, please just give me a call.

or

You shouldn't have any problems at all with this smoke detector, but if you do, please let me know. I'd be glad to help out.

I have never understood this strategy. My theory is this: Customers are in a strange state of mind immediately after making any purchase; they're very impressionable; they'll do nearly anything you or anyone else tells them to do at that moment. If you suggest they will have problems, they'll make sure they do. If you suggest they'll have questions, they'll make some up.

Why not just tell them to enjoy their purchase? If you've made any kind of impression on the customer at all as a professional, it should go without saying that you'll handle any problems that might arise or that you'll always be available to answer their questions. Take advantage of their special state of mind in a positive way instead. For example, if you told one of your customers, "Go home and enjoy your new CDs this afternoon," he might just do it.

Making the Proper Invitation

With the invitation process, you are literally inviting your customers back to the store. But I don't mean saying something as cliched as "Thanks and come again soon!" This is not the time to try and drum up extra business. It is the time to sincerely thank the customers and invite them to come back and share their joy with the item. Remember, it's a CELEBRATION OF THANKS. But, of course, when they do come back—you might as well sell them something else!

An invitation, which follows the confirmation of the sale, is carefully worded according to the customer's specific situation. For example, if Mrs. Woods bought her husband a home computer from your store, you might ask her to return to the store next time she's in the area to let you know how her husband liked it or how surprised he was that she picked it out for him, etc.

Here are some guidelines for successfully inviting your customers back to your store:

1. Make an agreement with your customers. By beginning the invitation with "Will you do me a favor?" you have made an agreement with the customer to return to your store.

How many times have you said "Yes" to someone who's asked you to do something, and then regretted it after hearing what the favor was? Still, you upheld the agreement anyway. It's one of the most wondrous aspects of human nature!

Most customers are the same way. They will say "Yes" and commit themselves to you in advance of knowing what the favor actually is. Don't assume, however, that the answer will be "Yes" and that you can proceed to the next step without actually getting your answer. While the answer will be "Yes" 99 percent of the time, exercise common courtesy and wait for a response.

2. Invite the customer back to the store to see *you*. Once you have gotten your customer to say "Yes" to your request for a favor, then ask the customer to come

back to the store to see you for a specific reason. The most practical reason for getting customers to come back is so that they may have the opportunity to let you know how their purchase has worked out or whether the person for whom they bought it was pleased.

Ideally, you want to also invite the person for whom the gift was purchased back to the store as well. If they're happy with their gift, then they might also be happy with some of the other merchandise in your store...and more amenable to spending their own money there.

Make your invitation as specific as possible: "Next time you're downtown, will you stop by and let me know how the engagement ring worked out? I'd really love to hear."

I've even gotten more specific than that: "I want to see you back in here by the end of next week so you can let me know how much she loved it. I can hardly wait any longer than that to find out!" Don't be afraid to test your customers' limits. Rarely will they say "No" once you've asked them to do you a personal favor.

As always, there are some extra considerations in making your invitation as effective as possible. Take a look at the following example:

Mr. Woods, I think you bought a wonderful ring. It's a gorgeous design and will go well with any style of wedding ring. Will you do me a special favor?

What's wrong here? The word "bought" is best left out of the confirmation process! If it's an expensive item, it's practically the same thing as saying ,"I think you made a great choice in buying this ring with all of your hard-earned money." Say instead the word "selected" or "chose."

Here's another consideration to keep in mind when making the invitation to your customer:

Salesperson: Miss Williams, I think you made the right choice in selecting this dress. Not only does it look adorable on you, but it can also be worn throughout the entire year. Would you do me a special favor?

202

Customer:	Okay.
Salesperson:	Next time you're in the mall, stop by and let us know how you're doing. We'd love to see you.

What's wrong here? The salesperson did not personally invite the customer back! He simply asked the customer to come back to the store, not to see anyone in particular. What's the point if you're not going to make sure the customer comes back to see you? This is your golden opportunity to build your own personal trade.

Putting It All Together

As you might have guessed already, confirmations and invitations go together. If done properly, they can be beautiful music to a customer's ears! Here is an example of the complete confirmation and invitation process:

Salesperson:	Bob, I think you made the right choice in selecting this business phone system. The LED display will really make it easy for everyone in the office to learn to use and the flexibility to move phones from one station to another should be a great relief to your office manager, too. Would you do me a favor?
Customer:	Sure.
Salesperson:	Next time you're visiting the shopping center, would you stop by and let me know how well the system's working out for you? I'd love to hear.
Customer:	I will. Thanks for all your help.
Salesperson:	It was my pleasure.

BUILDING PERSONAL TRADE

You may call yourself a salesperson, but you're a businessperson, too. To be successful, you've got to develop client relationships and work every day on maintaining and expanding them.

In short: Sell like an ace, and act like an entrepreneur.

Tapping Your Entrepreneurial Spirit

Retail sales is a process as entrepreneurial as the one performed by the guy down the street who opens his own printing shop. He's got to keep track of all his current and prospective customers so that he can let them know when a new piece of printing equipment arrives or when a new stock of paper is available. His livelihood depends upon his customer outreach efforts. If he doesn't let them know he's in business, few will find out.

Although you may work in an area with a consistent flow of buyer traffic, it's never a good idea to wait for the customers to come to you. That's lazy salesmanship. One of my favorite sales mottos is:

A salesperson's work is never done.

Even after customers walk out of the store, you still need to be thinking about that sale. If they are new customers, write down all the information you have about them, including their name, address, phone number, interests, date of purchase, and items purchased.

Think about what you'll attempt to sell those customers next time they are in your store, or how you will get in touch with them if they don't return to your store within the next few weeks. If they are repeat customers, be sure to update your customer file with similar information.

Getting to Know the Customer

If you're going to go to the trouble of inviting customers back to the store, you need to know what you're going to do with them once they've returned. Customers like personal attention and having other people worry about them. If you can demonstrate that you know what that person's needs and desires are, then you are likely to earn yourself a devoted customer.

In recent years, personalized shopping services have proliferated as women and other professionals have found their leisure time increasingly limited. These are private consultants who are making good money doing shopping for their clients! Some of these people are experts, some of them aren't. Some of them probably wander around the mall as aimlessly as their clients do.

So why not think of yourself as a private consultant, too? You're the expert regarding your store's particular merchandise, right? Learn to be a private consultant to all your customers.

Position yourself as the person to whom customers come for advice, and upon whom they can rely to help them select the items they may need or desire.

Many Approaches to Help Build Personal Trade

I recommend using a variety of methods to keep your name in front of your customers. With every method, you can begin to achieve the goal of personal trade:

1. Getting to the customers you want to reach, and
2. Telling them about YOU.

It's not only the store and its merchandise you're selling, it's you and your ability and knowledge as a caring salesperson! Demonstrate your concern through as many of the following six methods as possible:

1. Send thank-you notes to all of your customers. I recommend personal, handwritten notes to all of your customers regardless of how much they spent in your store. Make them short and sweet: "Thanks for shopping with me. I hope you enjoy it." It's not necessary to sell anything else or invite them back to the store.

So few salespeople send out thank-you notes anyway that you're going to stand out among the crowd simply by saying, "Thank you." I even recall hearing somewhere that most people can remember all of the thank-you cards they've received in the last five years and who sent them!

Start this process today! Send out thank-you notes to all the customers who purchased something from you today. Who knows, one or more of those customers may return to the store and thank you for your thank-you card!

2. Make follow-up phone calls or send follow-up notes. Get back in touch with all of your customers within three months of their last purchase (or less, if appropriate). Again, make it short and sweet. All you want to do here is let the customer know about some new merchandise that has arrived in the store that you think would complement the items that have already been purchased: "Thanks for shopping with me last month. Some new silk scarves have arrived that would complement your new dress beautifully. Just thought you would like to know."

Whatever you do, you're offering a reminder to your customer about your services and the variety of merchandise you have in your store.

3. Send "FYI" correspondence. Pretend you sell water purifiers and you recently sold a large volume of them to a developer who plans to install them in a new neighborhood of homes he's building. The next month, you're reading an article in a trade magazine about the popularity of water purifiers among homeowners. Wouldn't it be a great idea to photocopy this article and send it to the customer who recently made an investment in your store?

Sending "FYI" correspondence can be a tremendous sales tool for retail salespeople. If it's an article from a trade magazine or other publication, it's a third-party endorsement of the product the customer purchased from your store. Another confirmation! Better yet, the "FYI" correspondence doesn't attempt to sell anything and is therefore perceived as valuable product information.

In sending out your "FYI" correspondence, simply hand-write a brief note in the corner of the copy or on your business card that says something like: "I thought you might be interested in this. Best wishes, Susie Salesperson."

4. Send holiday cards to your customers. You can send your customers holiday cards for a variety of occasions. It's just one more good excuse to keep in touch. All you have to do is sign your name and say "hello." Your customers will appreciate you thinking of them.

However, before you rush out to buy a sleigh full of Christmas cards, think about your true purpose. You want to get someone's attention, right? So why send a customer a Christmas card when practically everyone else they know or buy from is going to be sending one, too? Yours will only get lost in the mass of others.

Instead, use your imagination; send out your holiday cards for odd occasions, such as:

- Groundhog's Day
- Valentine's Day
- St. Patrick's Day
- Halloween
- July 4th

One good idea is to announce the start of each new clothing season with cards announcing the beginning of the season, whether it be spring, summer, fall or winter. In this way, you can alert your customers to the fact that the newest merchandise for that particular season is in.

If you worry about appearing strange to a customer who receives a St. Patrick's Day card from you, don't. The whole point is to be different and make an impression. Be exciting and memorable; don't be dull and forgettable.

5. Send a birthday card to the merchandise. Here's another way to be creative with your follow-up techniques. Don't send a birthday card to your customer. (It will only get lost in the shuffle with all of the others they receive, or seem too slick.)

Send a birthday card announcing the birthday of the merchandise your customer purchased from your store. Or rather, let the customer know that you're celebrating the anniversary of the purchase of that particular item. If you sold a customer a watch, a typical birthday card might read: "Dear Mr. Jones, I wanted to let you know that your watch is one year old today. Congratulations! Next time you're in the mall, why don't you bring it by for a visit? We'd love to see how it's doing. By now, it could probably use a good cleaning to keep it looking sharp!"

6. Send your own personal newsletter. Of my six favorite ways to build personal trade, this is probably my most favorite. That's because few of your competitors will take the time to do a personal newsletter, even though it adds a special touch to your personal presentation as a salesperson and helps to establish your authority in your respective field of retail.

A personal newsletter, however, does not have to be incredibly time-consuming or expensive. All you have to do is prepare one 8-1/2 × 11-inch sheet of paper on your typewriter or computer—whatever you have available that produces decent type. Get an estimate for typesetting the piece twice a year; you may find that it's a minimal expense that you can afford.

Place your own photo and the name of your store in the top left hand corner of the newsletter, and use the column space to talk about trends in the business. This copy can be from your own perspective, or it can be borrowed from an article in a trade magazine that tracks such trends. (Remember to give credit if you borrow another writer's work.) You can also take this opportunity to inform your select group of customers about new merchandise the store has received.

I know one department store salesperson who not only distributed a personal newsletter to talk about what was "hot" and what was not, she also used the space to talk about her participation in the store's charitable activities. By doing so, this salesperson generated an incredible amount of goodwill within the community and enhanced her credibility as a caring, sensitive person and devoted member of the community.

Customers learned to like her though her charitable efforts and always looked for her when they came into the store. Many real estate agents, in fact, distribute personal newsletters to talk about their particular neighborhoods or areas of specialty. This may include discussions of what's sold in the neighborhood, what is currently on the market, and what new changes are going on in the marketplace.

A Retail Success Story

One of the most successful retail saleswomen I know once told me that she makes it a habit to *follow up with every single customer* who walks into her store's dress department. She said she does this by keeping track of every customer's visit and writing it all down in what she calls a "client book." In this book, she records the following information on the customer:

- Date of visit
- Name and address
- Home and business phone
- Occupation
- Preferred method of payment
- Preferred vendors and fabric colors
- Purchase activity
- Birthday or other special events

This saleswoman told me that by recording all of this information (which may seem tedious and time-consuming), she is able to establish person-to-person relationships with all of her customers. "People come in to see me, not to see what's behind the window display in our store," she said.

Once a relationship has been established with a particular customer, this saleswoman makes a point to call or send personal notes. She even encourages "appointment shopping" for many of her clients, a process whereby the client calls ahead to make an appointment and the saleswoman then arranges her schedule so that she can spend up to 30 minutes alone with that particular customer.

During this time, she may show the customer new merchandise or help the customer select new accessories for a previously purchased item. This service, the saleswoman said, is ideal for customers with busy schedules.

If you find that one of your customers regularly needs special attention or has limited time to shop, offer to be accommodating. If you were a customer, wouldn't you be impressed if someone took a special interest in you? And wouldn't you buy more from this person? Or course you would.

To Recapitulate

Every customer who walks into your store also walks in with the power to return whatever was purchased. Therefore, be careful not to buy back the sale. Learn to cement every sale by confirming your customers' purchases and by letting them know *they* made the right decision. It may take a while for the results to start to pay off, but believe me—it makes a difference.

Finally, use the invitations process as a means of getting customers back into your store and developing your own personal trade. Take care of your customers, and they'll begin to take care of you.

HOT TIPS AND KEY INSIGHTS

- Throw yourself into each and every sale, and don't assume the sale is over because you've rung up the register or deposited the money.

- Position yourself not only as an authority in your field, but also as a resource for your customers. Work with your clients, follow up with them and they'll gradually begin to consider you a personal assistant.

- Before you get ready to celebrate your next sale, make sure the sale is final. Although you may complete all the necessary steps leading up to and including the close, you may not have "cemented" the sale. Confirming the sale helps to prevent buyer's remorse.

- Your job is to ask for the sale and to reassure customers about their purchase once the sale is final: you have the unique opportunity to be the first person to let the customer know that he or she made the right choice.

- After the transaction is complete, you are no longer a salesperson, you are just another human being in a store. Therefore, complimentary remarks from you will be taken as compliments, rather than as typical sales remarks.

- For more meaningful confirmations use the customer's name, and use "I" and "you." This helps to further personalize the exchange. It's not the store that's thanking the customer, it's you. And you want to be sure to give that customer credit for making the wise buying decision. Think of this whole process as a "celebration of thanks," and be specific about the purchase.

- In the case of expensive items, like diamonds, cars or watches, make a phone call confirmation. If you make confirmation phone calls every night to your customers, you can significantly reduce your rate of customer returns and cancellations.

- Salespeople who regularly earn in the six-figure salary range aren't just lucky—they get their customers to come back to *them*. It's far easier to sell to a repeat or referral customer than to a new one.

- The key to the invitation process is to tailor your request to the customers' situations so that they become "obligated" to let you know how they (or their friend or family member) enjoy the items you just sold. When the satisfied customer or friend or family member returns to your store, you have created a wonderful opportunity to sell more merchandise.

- The most practical reason for getting customers to come back is so that they can tell you how their purchase has worked out or whether the person for whom they bought it was pleased. Ideally, you want to invite the person for whom the gift was purchased back to the store as well.

- Don't tell your customers to have problems. Many salespeople tell their customers to watch out for problems they may have with the merchandise: "Thanks again. If you have any problems with your new stove-top grill, let me know!"

- Even after the customer walks out of the store, you still need to be thinking about that sale. If it's a new customer, write down all the information you have about that customer, including name, address, telephone number, interests, date of purchase, and items purchased. Think about what you'll attempt to sell that customer next time he or she is in your store, or how you will get in touch if that customer doesn't return to your store within the next few weeks.

- Learn to be a private consultant to your customers. Position yourself as the one to whom they all need to come for advice and upon whom they can rely to help them select the items they may need or desire.

- Use a variety of methods to keep your name in front of your customers. With every method, you can begin to achieve the goals of personal trade: getting to the customers you want to reach, and telling them about YOU.

- Every customer who walks into your store also walks in with the power to return whatever he or she bought. Therefore, be careful not to buy back the sale. Learn to cement every sale by confirming your customers' purchases and by letting them know *they* made the right decision. Use the invitation process as a means of getting customers back into your store and developing some sort of personal trade.

FINAL THOUGHTS

Did you have fun? I sure hope so. When I get out there on the floor, it never fails to be a game worth playing. And when you win—WOW! Not only do you take the spoils, but the store and most important, your customer, will win as well.

Having a career in sales has had its mixed blessings. For years I was embarrassed that I had not become a lawyer, doctor or some other "professional." I really had no skill to speak of and it seemed I was destined to be one in the crowd. Then it happened. I decided to learn more about selling and give it a go.

Today I feel I can truly call myself a professional. Selling is something that I not only care about but has become a passion. And it is something I know I do very well. There are not many areas in my life where I can call myself an expert or a professional. Selling has given me a sense of accomplishment.

You, too, have that choice and chance. You don't need to go to college but you do have to become a student. You don't have to work at the best place, but you do have to work to be the best. You don't need a million dollar customer, but you do have to treat each one like a million dollars. And most important of all, you have to want to be successful.

I am very proud to say that this selling system is the most-used system of retail selling in the world. Maybe because it has a lot of "how to." Maybe because it has been put together in a logical sequence of steps. Or maybe because it was born out of experiences on the selling floor that make it easy to relate to. I know that if you give the information contained in this book a real chance, the techniques and strategies you will discover will turn many more of your shoppers into buyers.

From the daily precheck to confirmations and invitations, you will find that I have tried not to waste your time with techniques that you will find hard to accomplish or that you won't enjoy.

Treat each step as a goal. Once accomplished, move on to the next step. You will find, by treating each step in this way, that it will be a lot easier to reach the final result you are looking for—sales.

And finally, customer service is best accomplished by selling honestly and lovingly. Your customers will continue to have a choice of where to shop. Treated poorly, they go away in groups and have to be earned back one at a time. And don't forget, it's always SHOWTIME!

About the Author...

HARRY J. FRIEDMAN
Retail Consultant, Trainer, Speaker and Author

"You don't meet Harry J. Friedman – you encounter him. He's outrageous, revolutionary, inventive and invigorating. His unique style shakes you up and forces you to rethink the way you sell or manage on a retail floor. Then he blows you away with scores of why-didn't-I-think-of-that techniques for turning more of your shoppers into buyers. If his vision of how a retail store should run could be bottled and delivered to every retailer in the world, retailing would be elevated to heights it has never seen."
– Retail Executive

Harry J. Friedman is an internationally acclaimed consultant specializing in retail sales and management. Since 1968, he has established himself as a super-salesman, record-breaking sales manager, owner of a successful chain of retail stores, and trainer of more than 250,000 retailers.

His unique ability to share his experience in a clear and motivating manner has made him the most heavily attended speaker and most widely read author on retail sales and management in the world. Known for his entertaining but hard-hitting style, he delivers volumes of real-life, here's-how information that go far beyond motivation.

He is the creator of retail's number one sales and management system – used by more retailers than any other system of its kind in the world. To his credit are articles published more than 500 times in national trade magazines and the "On The Floor" retail newsletter, regularly read by over 75,000 retailers. He has also developed retail's most heavily attended store management seminars: the Retail Management Training Camp, Multiple Store Supervision Course, and Retail Employee Development Course – which offer proven techniques for recruiting, hiring, motivating, training, managing, compensating and retaining top retail producers.

Training products he has contributed include the recently updated Friedman Professional Retail Selling Course. The warmth and spirit captured in this video training program not only brings many of the pages of this book to life, but make it the perfect tool for training both rookie and veteran salespeople. Among other of his numerous training products are the Management Training Program, Retailer's Complete Book of Selling Games & Contests, Retail Policies Manual and ever-expanding Retail Productivity Series.

Mr. Friedman's special talent for de-mystifying retail's most puzzling sales and management issues has made him the most talked about and sought-after consultant in the industry today. Not one to rest on his laurels, he continues to sharpen his skills as he works with single store independents to mega-store giants, trade associations, manufacturers and Fortune 500 companies around the world. As president and founder of The Friedman Group, his dedication to increasing retail productivity and professionalism, have earned him a place as retail's foremost authority.

The Friedman Group was founded in 1980 to provide retailers with a way to professionally train and manage their people. All sales and management programs offered have been compiled by a staff whose strong retail experience has allowed them to turn theoretical concepts into practical, usable, "here's-how" systems that work where it really counts – on your sales floor and in your cash register. Responsible for millions of dollars in sales increases for some of the largest, and smallest, retailers in the world, The Friedman Group is retail's sales and management training resource.

RETAIL TRAINING RESOURCES

The following programs are recommended to complement this book and enhance the productivity and professionalism of your staff.

**Retail Sales & Management Books,
Audio & Video Training Programs**

Friedman Professional Retail Selling Course: The most widely-used video sales training system in retail brings the excitement of a live Harry J. Friedman sales seminar right into your store. Teach your staff all the steps for getting past customer resistance, probing for bigger sales, routinely adding on, closing the sale and developing a steady stream of repeat business. 9 videos – including industry-specific role plays, 5 participant's workbooks, and 1 leader's guide. Accompanying Certification Program comes with coach's video, coach's guide and 5 checksheet booklets, and guarantees each salesperson can apply what they've learned on the sales floor.

Retailer's Complete Book of Selling Games & Contests: Over 100 on-the-floor selling games, contests and variations, guaranteed to motivate your salespeople, improve their selling skills and immediately generate more sales. The perfect tool for getting your staff excited about selling and turning a slow sales week into a quota-busting sales record. 250 page manual, plus video overview featuring Harry J. Friedman, and 3 full-color reusable game boards.

Management Training Program: *Just-Updated Live Recording!* International retail authority Harry J. Friedman presenting the highly-acclaimed Retail Management Training Camp. Learn how to motivate your staff and bring a passion for selling to your sales floor, how to set individual and store sales goals and see that they're met, how objectively holding your salespeople accountable for their sales will increase the quantity and quality of their sales, how to create a culture of great customer service, and more. 12 audio tapes plus 263 page manual with reproducible forms, checklists and reference material.

Retail Employee Development Course: *New Live Recording!* Retail's hottest new 3-day seminar presented in a condensed 4-hour version by Harry J. Friedman. Discover how to recruit, hire, train and retain top-producing retail employees. How to go from "frantically searching" to "selectively choosing" the best person for the job, and how to pinpoint the kind of salesperson that you should be hiring for your store. Learn how to build a training "system" instead of just training people, and discover what causes employees to stay and contribute to your success. 6 audio tapes, plus 258 page comprehensive course manual.

Multiple Store Supervision Course: *New Live Recording!* Retail's only district management seminar comes right to you in this compact 4-hour audio program for busy executives. Harry J. Friedman offers up proven techniques for effectively managing multiple stores and increasing productivity. Find out how to go from continually putting out daily fires to eliminating non-compliance and building better store managers. Learn why some stores lag behind the rest and how to bring them quickly up to speed, how often to visit your stores and what to do when you're there, and how to set up a "model" store that becomes the standard for all stores to follow. Complete training program includes 6 audio tapes plus 253 page course manual.

Retail Policies Manual: The first easy-to-customize store policies manual. Sample policies researched to be the most commonly used in retail today, along with points to consider in establishing the right policies for your store, are provided in a deluxe 3-ring binder. Sample manual on computer disk (for IBM or MAC) makes it simple to revise and create your own manual.

Retail Customer Service On Trial: _New Video Program!_ The courtroom drama that challenges your staff to examine customer service from both sides of the sales counter.

In "The People vs. Acme Retail," a store owner, manager and salesperson take the stand against claims of "gross negligence in customer service," as six customers testify against them. This mock trial was video-taped in realistic courtroom fashion and contains familiar, sometimes hilarious retail scenarios that everyone can identify with. Watch your staff take sides and then rethink how they're treating their own customers, as they join the jury in seeking justice for all on the retail floor. Great for store meetings and informal training sessions. 45-minute video, leader's guide and full trial transcript.

Satisfying Difficult Customers: _New Video Program!_ Ever had a difficult customer? How you handle that person can either be frustrating or satisfying, and plays a large role in whether or not you make the sale. This fascinating program by Harry J. Friedman will reveal what many salespeople do to cause customers to be difficult, and shows you how to avoid these all-too-common mistakes. Learn techniques like the "Iceberg Theory" to spot potentially volatile situations, and how to diffuse irritated customers with a simple three-word phrase and supportive body language that works like a charm. Instead of chalking up that missed sale to dealing with another tough customer, learn how to turn that adversary into one of your best customers. 45-minute video, 5 participant's workbooks and 1 comprehensive leader's guide.

Team Selling – _Working Together To Close More Sales_: _New Video Program!_ How many times have salespeople in your store missed a sale because they just couldn't connect with the customer? And how many times could that sale have been saved, if it was turned over to another salesperson, before the customer turned for the door? Retail authority Harry J. Friedman reveals how "team selling," or turning over the sale to another salesperson, can dramatically increase sales and customer satisfaction. Learn to recognize customer signals that say it's time to turn over (T.O.) the sale, and step-by-step techniques for making T.O.s go smoothly and successfully. Team selling will show you how to make the most of every opportunity and prevent sales from walking out the door. 45-minute video, 5 participant's workbooks and 1 comprehensive leader's guide.

Harry J. Friedman on Retail Selling & Management: Live audio recordings offer a fascinating overview of the philosophies behind the retail sales and management system that has caused millions of dollars in sales increases. 2 audio tapes with written transcripts each.

How to Legally Hire & Fire: Everyone in your company involved in hiring, disciplining or firing, must know what's legal and effective. Nationally acclaimed labor relations attorney Charles H. Goldstein will tell you what you can and can't ask in interviews, how to avoid discrimination and wrongful discharge suits, how to legally discipline and more. 2 video tapes and comprehensive manuals.

Retail Store Management Seminars

Retail Management Training Camp: _Retail's #1 Seminar!_ The store management seminar attended by owners, supervisors and managers representing well over 50,000 stores, will show you how to manage, motivate and train your retail staff to immediately produce more sales. Learn how to run your store, instead of letting your store run you. Discover how to get total control over daily store operations, develop a goal-oriented staff and keep them producing at record sales levels. Learn to hold your salespeople accountable for their sales, and easily track sales performance. Find out how to coach your staff when sales drop or level off, and much more. 3-day seminar includes comprehensive 263 page manual, with ready-to-use forms, checklists and reference material. Call for dates and locations near you.

Multiple Store Supervision Course: _Just Updated!_ The first district store management seminar that shows owners, area supervisors and district managers how to manage multiple locations and increase productivity. You'll learn how hitting your sales goals as a district or company is reliant on building stores individually, how to project sales goals and notice trends, the importance of creating a "model store," how to effectively staff your stores and stop settling for average employees, how to eliminate non-compliance, how going from district cop to district leader gets respect and results, and much more. 3-day seminar includes comprehensive 253 page manual, with ready-to-use forms, checklists and reference material. Call for dates and locations in your area.

Retail Employee Development Course: _New! Retail's Hottest Topics!_ The seminar that gives you proven techniques for recruiting, hiring, training, compensating and retaining top retail producers. You'll discover how to set up a recruiting system that provides a ready supply of potential employees, how to hire the right person – one who can add an extra $50,000 to $250,000 to your annual sales, how to develop performance-based compensation packages that stimulate productivity and retain top producers, how to keep customers coming back because of the way you train your staff to serve them, and how to cause employees to stay and contribute to your success. 3-day seminar includes comprehensive 300+ page manual, with ready-to-use forms, checklists and reference material. Call for upcoming seminar dates and locations.

In-House Training

Bring our training to your location. The Friedman Group can deliver all or part of the above seminars, as well as retail sales training, in cost-effective in-house programs that can be designed to fit your schedule. Programs can vary in length from one hour to several days.

Project Gold Star™ - "Getting It Done" Retail Productivity Implementation Program: _New!_ Let our senior consultants guide you through the complete implementation of our retail store management system, in a series of monthly two-day meetings held over four consecutive months. Limited to just 15 companies, each session includes portions of our three store management courses, but delivered in greater detail than is covered in our public seminars. Key to the program is the opportunity to come back to subsequent meetings and get answers to your implementation questions, and the ability to have a model of the entire system up and running in just four months. Call for upcoming dates and locations.

On Track™ Retail Productivity Improvement Programs: You'll never really know how successful your stores can be until the most important parts of your business are On Track. This comprehensive Retail Productivity Improvement Program brings one of our training specialists to your company for in-store needs assessment, expert training and customized implementation of our sales and/or management systems. Included is a full complement of our training products and seminar tickets, all packaged together at greatly reduced prices. Call your Friedman Group representative to learn how this program can make the most of your most valuable resource – your people – and take you from mildly successful to *wildly* successful.

Professional Speakers: *"The chicken was dry, but the speaker was sensational!"* Whatever the need – keynote address, annual meeting, trade show, seminar or hands-on workshop – we'll make your next event a long-remembered success. The Friedman Group's professional speakers aren't just experts, but RETAIL experts. They are all polished speakers with extensive retail backgrounds and first-hand experience implementing the Friedman System in the real world. No canned or boring speeches that don't relate, you'll get a lot more than the hoped for "one good idea." Count on them for presentations that are as motivating and entertaining as they are educational.

Consulting & Customized Training Programs

The Friedman Group provides consulting and customized training programs for large and small retailers, trade associations and manufacturers in the areas of sales, customer service, store management, operations and product knowledge, as well as developing customized policies and procedures manuals. Using our expert trainers, in-house writing staff, video studio and edit bay, we can create and help implement the perfect training tools for your company – in a very cost effective manner. Put your thumbprint on your retail training. Call to learn why so many successful companies rely on The Friedman Group for their retail training resource.

For more information on the above and additional retail training resources...

CALL 800-351-8040
310-645-7355 or FAX 310-645-6241

The Friedman Group
P.O. Box 92003, Los Angeles, CA 90009, U.S.A.
United States • South America • Australia • New Zealand
• South Africa • Europe